HEMPHER

CONFESSIONS
OF A
BRITISH SPY

and

British Enmity
Against Islam

Published by Omnia Veritas Ltd

contact@omniaveritas.org

www.omnia-veritas.com

Table of Contents

Part I

HEMPHER

Preface

Allâhu ta'âlâ declared in the eighty-second âyat of **Mâida soûra** of Qur'ân al-kerîm, "The biggest enemies of Islam are the Jews and mushriks." The first mischief contrived to demolish Islam from within was instigated by a Jew, namely Abdullah bin Sebe' of Yemen. He established the Shiite sect against the **Ahl as-sunna,** the true Muslim group. From then on, Jews under the cloak of Shiite scholars in every century consolidated this sect. After the Ascension of 'Îsâ 'alaihissalâm' a number of corrupt Bibles were written. Most of the Christians became **mushriks** (those who believe in more than one god). Others became **kâfirs** (disbelievers) since they did not believe Muhammad 'alaihissalâm'. These and the Jews were called **Ahl-i kitâb** (people with a heavenly book). When Islam was established, the hegemony of the priests, as in the Dark Ages, was abolished. They founded missionary organizations to abolish Islam. The British were the forerunners in this regard. **A Ministry of the Commonwealth** was established in London with a view to fighting against Islam. People who worked in this Ministry were taught the Jewish tricks. Contriving inconceivably vicious plans, they attacked Islam using all available military and political forces toward this end.

Hempher, only one of the thousands of male and female agents employed and sent forth to all countries by this ministry, entrapped a person named Muhammad of Najd in Basra, misled him for several years, and caused him to establish the sect called **Wahhâbî** in

1125 [1713 A.D.]. They announced this sect in 1150.

Hempher is a British missioner who was assigned the task of carrying on espionage activities in Egypt, Iraq, Iran, Hidjaz and in Istanbul, the center of the (Islamic) caliphate, misleading Muslims and serving Christianity, by means of the Ministry of British Commonwealth of Nations. No matter how assiduously the enemies of Islam may strive to annihilate Islam, they will never be able to extinguish this light of Allâhu ta'âlâ. For Allâhu ta'âlâ declares as follows, as purported in the twelfth and sixty-third âyats of Yûsuf sûra and in the ninth âyat of Hijr sûra of Qur'ân al-kerîm: **"I have revealed this Qur'ân to thee. Verily I shall be its protector."** Disbelievers will not be able to desecrate it, change it or defile it. They shall never extinguish that light. Allâhu ta'âlâ sent Qur'ân al-kerîm to His beloved Prophet Muhammad 'alaihis-salâm' piece by piece in twenty-three years through His angel named Jebrâ'îl. Abû Bekr "radiyallâhu ta'âlâ 'anh", the first Khalîfa, had the 6236, âyats which were sent by Allâhu ta'âlâ, compiled, and thus the great book named **Mushaf** was formed. Muhammad 'alaihis-salâm' explained the whole Qur'ân al-kerîm to his As-hâb.

The Islamic scholars wrote down whatever they heard from the As-hâb-i-kirâm. Thousands of books of tafsîr (explanation) thus formed were published in every country. All copies of Qur'ân al-kerîm existent throughout the world today are identical. There is not even a single literal or diacritical difference in any of them. For fourteen centuries Muslims worked in the lightsome way taught by Qur'ân al-kerîm and made progress in knowledge, in ethics, in science, arts, trade, and politics. They established great States. After the French Revolution in 1204 [C.E. 1789], European youth saw the immoralities, cruelties, robberies and mendacities being perpetrated by churches and priests, and, as a result, some of them became Muslims, while others turned into atheists. The farther away from Christianity, the more progress they made in science and technology. For Christianity was an impediment to worldly endeavours and progress. And some Muslims, reading the books written by these young people in order to criticize Christianity, and believing the lies and slanders which the British missionaries directed against Islam, became quite ignorant of Islam. As they were alienated from Islam, they began to decline in science. For one of the principal commandments of Islam is to work for worldly progress.

The British state policy is essentially based on methods of exploiting the natural riches of the world, particularly those in Africa and India, employing their inhabitants like beasts, and transferring all the resultant revenue to Britain. People who have had the fortune of attaining Islam, the religion which commands justice, mutual love and charity, pose an obstruction athwart to British cruelties and falsities.

We have prepared this book of ours in three sections:

The first section, which consists of seven parts, comprises the slanders of the British spy. They were designed by the British for the purpose of annihilating Islam.

The second section relates how the British insidiously put their treacherous plans into practice in Muslim countries, how they deceived statesmen, how they inflicted unimaginably bitter torments on Muslims, and how they destroyed the Indian and the Ottoman States. How the Jews and the British attacked Islam is reported with quotations from **Hakîkat-ul-Yehûd,** which was written by Fuâd bin Abdurrahman Rufâî and published by Mektebetussahâbetul Islamiyye in Kuwait-Safât-Salimiyya. This section of our book is corroborated with documents which will awaken those poor Muslims who are entrapped by the Wahhabis and will support the writings of the scholars of the Ahl as-sunna.

Chapter I

Hempher says:

Our Great Britain is very vast. The sun rises over its seas, and sets, again, below its seas. Yet our state is relatively weak concerning its colonies in India, China and Middle East. These countries are not entirely under our domination. However, we have been carrying on a very active and successful policy in these places. We shall be in full possession of all of them very soon. Two things are of importance:

1- To try to retain the places we have already obtained;

2- To try to take possession of those places we have not obtained yet.

The Ministry of the Commonwealth assigned a commission from each of the colonies for the execution of these two tasks. As soon as I joined the Ministry of the Commonwealth, the Minister put his trust in me and appointed me the administrator of our company in East India. Outwardly it was a trade company. But its real task was to search for ways of taking control of the very vast lands of India.

Our government was not at all nervous about India. India was a country where people from various nationalities, speaking different languages, and having contrasting interests lived together. Nor were we afraid of China. For the religions dominant in China were Buddhism and Confucianism, neither of which was much of a threat. Both of them were dead religions that instituted no concern for life and which were no more than forms of addresses. For this reason, the people living in these two countries were hardly likely to have any feelings of patriotism. These two countries did not worry us, the British government. Yet the events that might occur later were not out of consideration for us. Therefore, we were designing long term plans to wage discord, ignorance, poverty, and even diseases in these countries. We were imitating the customs and traditions of these two countries, thus easily concealing our intentions.

What frazzled our nerves most was the Islamic countries. We had already made some agreements, all of which were to our advantage, with the Sick Man (the Ottoman Empire). Experienced members of the Ministry of the Commonwealth predicted that this sick man would pass away in less than a century. In addition, we had made some secret agreements with the Iranian government and placed in these two countries statesmen whom we had made masons. Such corruptions as bribery, incompetent administration and inadequate religious education, which in its turn led to being occupied with pretty women and consequently to neglect of duty, broke the backbones of these two countries. In spite of all these, we were anxious that our activities should not yield the results we expected, for reasons I am going to cite below:

1- Muslims are extremely devoted to Islam. Every individual Muslim is as strongly attached to Islam as a priest or monk to Christianity, if not more. As it is known, priests and monks would rather die than give up Christianity. The most dangerous of such people are the Shiites in Iran. For they put down people who are not Shiites as disbelievers and foul. Christians are like noxious dirt according to Shiites. Naturally, one would do one's best to get rid of dirt. I once asked a Shiite this: Why do you look on Christians as such? The answer I was given was this: "The Prophet of Islam was a very wise person. He put Christians under a spiritual oppression in order to make them find the right way by joining Allah's religion, Islam. As a matter of fact, it is a State policy to keep a person found dangerous under a spiritual oppression until he pledges obedience. The dirt I am speaking about is not material; it is a spiritual oppression which is not peculiar to Christians alone. It involves Sunnites and all disbelievers. Even our ancient Magian Iranian ancestors are foul according to Shiites."

I said to him: "Well! Sunnites and Christians believe in Allah, in Prophets, and in the Judgement Day, too; why should they be foul, then?" He replied, "They are foul for two reasons: They impute mendacity to our Prophet, Hadrat Muhammad – may Allah protect us against such an act![1] And we, in response to this

---

[1] However, those who impute mendacity to our Prophet are Shi'ites and Christians. The deviating beliefs, words and dirty works of Shi'ites which do not conform with those of our Prophet and Qur'ân al-kerîm are written and refuted each in the books of Ahl-i sunnat such us **As- Sawaiq ul-muhrika, Tuhfa-i ithnâ ashariyya, Te'yîd-i Ahl-i Sunnat, Nâhiye, Ashab-i kirâm, Hujaj-i qat'iyye,** and **Milal wa Nihal.** The author of **Sawaiq** Ahmed ibni Hajar Mekkî died in Mekka in 974 [1566 A.D.]; **Tuhfa's** author Abdul 'Azîz died in Delhi in 1239 [1824 A.D.]; **Te'yîd's** author Imam-i Rabbânî Ahmad Fârûqî died in Serhend in 1034 [1624 A.D.], **Nâhiye's** author Abdul 'Azîz Ferhârevî died in 1239 [1824 A.D.]; **Ashab-i kirâm's** author Abdulhakim Arwâsî died in Ankara in 1362 [1943 A.D.]; **Hujaj's** author Abdullah Suweydî died in Baghdâd in 1174 [1760 A.D.]; **Milal's** author Muhammad Shihristânî died in Baghdâd in 548 [1154 A.D.].

atrocious imputation, follow the rule expressed in the saying, 'If a person torments you, you can torment him in return', and say to them: 'You are foul.' Secondly; Christians make offensive allegations about the Prophets of Allah. For instance, they say: Îsâ (Jesus) 'alaihis-salâm' drank alcohol. Because he was accursed, he was crucified."

In consternation, I said to the man that Christians did not say so. "Yes, they do," was the answer, "and you don't know. It is written so in the Holy Bible." I became quiet. For the man was right in the first respect, if not in the second respect. I did not want to continue the dispute any longer. Otherwise, they might be suspicious of me dressed in Islamic attire as I was. I therefore avoided such disputes.

2- Islam was once a religion of administration and authority. And Muslims were respected. It would be difficult to tell these respectable people that they are slaves now. Nor would it be possible to falsify the Islamic history and say to Muslims: The honour and respect you obtained at one time was the result of some (favourable) conditions. Those days are gone now, and they will never come back.

3- We were very anxious that the Ottomans and Iranians might notice our plots and foil them. Despite the fact that these two States had already been debilitated considerably, we still did not feel certain because they had a central government with property, weaponry, and authority.

4- We were extremely uneasy about Islamic

scholars. For the scholars of Istanbul and Al-adh-har, and the Iraqi and Damascene scholars were insurmountable obstacles against our objectives. For they were the kind of people who would never compromise their principles to the tiniest extent because they had turned against the transient pleasures and adornments of the world and fixed their eyes on the Paradise promised by Qur'ân al-kerîm. The people followed them. Even the Sultan was afraid of them. Sunnites were not so strongly adherent to scholars as were Shiites. For Shiites did not read books; they only recognized scholars, and did not show due respect to the Sultan. Sunnites, on the other hand, read books, and respected scholars and the Sultan.

We therefore prepared a series of conferences. Yet each time we tried we saw with disappointment that the road was closed for us. The reports we received from our spies were always frustrating, and the conferences came to naught. We did not give up hope, though. For we are the sort of people who have developed the habit of taking a deep breath and being patient.

The Minister himself, the highest priestly orders, and a few specialists attended one of our conferences. There were twenty of us. Our conference lasted three hours, and the final session was closed without reaching a fruitful conclusion. Yet a priest said, "Do not worry! For the Messiah and his companions obtained authority only after a persecution that lasted three hundred years. It is hoped that, from the world of the unknown, he will cast an eye on us and grant us the good luck of evicting the unbelievers, (he means Muslims), from their centers, be it three hundred years later. With a strong belief and long-term patience, we must arm ourselves! In order to obtain authority, we must take possession of all sorts of media, try all possible methods. We must try to spread Christianity among Muslims. It will be good for us to realize our goal, even if it will be after centuries. For fathers work for their children."

A conference was held, and diplomats and religious men from Russia and France as well as from England attended. I was very lucky. I, too, attended because I and the Minister were in very good terms. In the conference, plans of breaking Muslims into groups and making them abandon their faith and bringing them round to belief (Christianizing them) like in Spain were discussed. Yet the conclusions reached were not as had been expected. I have written about all the talks held in that conference in my book "Ilâ Melekût-il-Mesîh."

It is difficult to suddenly uproot a tree that has sent out its roots to the depths of the earth. But we must make hardships easy and overcome them. Christianity came to spread. Our Lord the Messiah promised us this. The bad conditions that the east and the west were in helped Muhammad. Those conditions being gone, have taken away the nuisances (he means Islam) that accompanied them. We observe with pleasure today that the situation has changed completely. As a result of the great works and endeavours of our ministry and other Christian governments, Muslims are on the decline now. Christians, on the other hand, are gaining ascendancy. It is time we retook the places we lost throughout the centuries. The powerful State of Great Britain pioneers this blessed task [of annihilating Islam].

Chapter II

In the Hijrî year 1122, C.E. 1710, the Minister of the Commonwealth sent me to Egypt, Iraq, Hidjaz and Istanbul to act as a spy and to obtain information necessary and sufficient for the breaking up of the Muslims. The Ministry appointed nine more people, full of agility and courage, for the same mission and at the same time. In addition to the money, information and maps we would need, we were given a list containing names of statesmen, scholars, and chiefs of tribes. I will never forget! When I said farewell to the secretary, he said, "The future of our state is dependent on your success. Therefore you should exert your utmost energy."

I set out on a voyage to Istanbul, the center of the Islamic caliphate. Besides my primary duty, I was to learn Turkish very well, the native language of the Muslims there. I had already learned in London a considerable amount of Turkish, Arabic (the language of the Qur'ân) and Persian, the language of Iranians. Yet learning a language was quite different from speaking that language like its native speakers. While the former skill can be acquired in a matter of a few years, the latter requires a duration of time several times as long as this. I had to learn Turkish with all its subtleties lest the people should suspect me.

I was not anxious that they should suspect me. For Muslims are tolerant, open-hearted, benevolent, as they have learnt from their Prophet Muhammad 'alai-his-salâm'. They are not sceptical like us. After all, at that time the Turkish government did not have an organization to arrest spies.

After a very tiresome voyage I arrived in Istanbul. I said my name was Muhammad and began to go to the mosque, Muslims' temple. I liked the way Muslims observed discipline, cleanliness and obedience. For a moment I said to myself: Why are we fighting these innocent people? Is this what our Lord Jesus Christ advised us? But I at once recovered from this diabolical [!] thought, and decided to carry out my duty in the best manner.

In Istanbul I met an old scholar named "Ahmed Efendi." With his elegant manners, open-heartedness, spiritual limpidity, and benevolence, none of our religious men I had seen could have equalled him. This person endeavoured day and night to make himself like the Prophet Muhammad. According to him, Muhammed was the most perfect, the highest man. Whenever he mentioned his name his eyes would become wet. I must have been very lucky, for he did not even ask who I was or where I was from. He would address me as "Muhammad Efendi." He would answer my questions and treat me with tenderness and with compassion. For he considered me a guest who had come to Istanbul to work in Turkey and to live in the shadow of the Khalîfa, the representative of the Prophet Muhammad. Indeed, this was the pretext I used to stay in Istanbul.

One day I said to Ahmed Efendi: "My parents are dead. I don't have any brothers or sisters, and I haven't inherited any property. I came to the center of Islam to work for a living and to learn Qur'ân al-kerîm and the Sunnat, that is, to earn both my worldly needs and my life in the Hereafter." He was very delighted with these words of mine, and said, "You deserve to be respected for these three reasons." I am writing down exactly what he said:

1.   "You are a Muslim. All Muslims are brothers.

2.   You are a guest. Rasûlullah 'sall-Allâhu alaihi wa sallam' declared: 'Offer kind hospitality to your guests!'

3.   You want to work. There is a hadîth-i sherîf stating that **'a person who works is beloved to Allah.'**"

These words pleased me very much. I said to myself, "Would that there were such bright truths in Christianity, too! It's a shame there aren't any." What surprised me was the fact that Islam, such a noble religion as it was, was being degenerated in the hands of these conceited people who were quite unaware of what was going on in life.

I said to Ahmed Efendi that I wanted to learn Qur'ân al- kerîm. He replied that he would teach me with pleasure, and began to teach me **(Fâtiha sûra).** He would explain the meanings as we read. I had great difficulty pronouncing some words. In two years' time I read through the whole Qur'ân al-kerîm. Before each lesson he would make an ablution and also command me to make an ablution. He would sit towards the qibla (Ka'ba) and then begin teaching.

What Muslims call ablution consisted of a series of washings, as follows:

1) Washing the face;
2) Washing the right arm from fingers to elbows;
3) Washing the left arm from fingers to elbows;
4) Making masah of (moistening both hands and rubbing them gently on) the head, backs of the ears, (back of) neck;
5) Washing both feet.

Having to use the miswâk vexed me very much. "Miswâk" is a twig with which they (Muslims) clean their mouth and teeth. I thought this piece of wood was harmful for the mouth and teeth. Sometimes it would hurt my mouth and cause bleeding. Yet I had to use it. For, according to them, using the "miswâk" was a muakkad sunnat of the Prophet. They said this wood was very useful. Indeed, the bleeding of my teeth came to an end. And the foul breath that I had had till that time, and which most British people have, was gone.

During my stay in Istanbul I spent the nights in a room I had rented from a man responsible for the service in a mosque. This servant's name was "Marwân Efendi". Marwân is the name of one of the Sahâba (Companions) of the Prophet Muhammad. The servant was a very nervous man. He would boast about his name and tell me that if I should have a son in the future I should "name him Marwân, because Marwân is one of Islam's greatest warriors."

"Marwân Efendi" would prepare the evening dinner. I would not go to work on Friday, a holiday for Muslims. On the other days of the week I worked for a carpenter named Khâlid, being paid on a weekly basis. Because I worked part time, i.e. from morning till noon, he would give me half the wage he gave the other employees. This carpenter would spend much of his free time telling about the virtues of "Khâlid bin Walîd". Khâlid bin Walîd, one of the Sahâba of the Prophet Muhammad, is a great mujâhid (a warrior for Islam). He accomplished various Islamic conquests. Yet his (Khâlid bin Walîd's) dismissal from office by 'Umar bin Hattâb during the latter's caliphate chafed the carpenter's heart.[2]

"Khâlid", the carpenter for whom I worked, was an immoral and extremely neurotic person. He somehow trusted me very much. I do not know why, but perhaps it was because I always obeyed him. He ignored the Sharî'at (Islam's commandments) in his secret manners. Yet when he was with his friends he would display obedience to the commandments of the Sharî'at. He would attend the Friday prayers, but I am not sure about the other (daily) prayers.

I would have breakfast in the shop. After work I would go to the mosque for early afternoon prayer and would stay there till late afternoon prayer. After late afternoon prayer I would go to Ahmed Efendi's place, where he would teach me such lessons as (reading) Qur'ân al-kerîm, Arabic and Turkish languages for two hours. Every Friday I would give him my weekly earnings because he taught me very well. Indeed, he taught me how to read Qur'ân al-kerîm very well, requirements of the Islamic religion and the subtleties

---

[2] When Ebû Ubayda bin Jerrâh, who was appointed in Khâlid bin Walîd's place, continued the conquests, it was realized that the reason for the conquests was the help of Allâhu ta'âlâ, not Khâlid himself.

of Arabic and Turkish languages.

When "Ahmed Efendi" knew that I was single, he wanted to marry me to one of his daughters. I refused his offer. But he insisted, saying that marriage is a sunnat of the Prophet's and that the Prophet had stated that **"A person who turns away from my sunnat is not of me."** Apprehending that this event might put an end to our personal dealings, I had to lie to him, saying that I lacked sexual power. Thus I ensured the continuance of our acquaintance and friendship.

When my two-year stay in Istanbul was over, I told "Ahmed Efendi" I wanted to go back home. He said, "No, don't go. Why are you going? You can find anything you might look for in Istanbul. Allâhu ta'âlâ has placed both the religion and the world at the same time in this city. You say that your parents are dead and you have no brothers or sisters. Why don't you settle down in Istanbul?..." "Ahmed Efendi" had formed a compulsive dependence upon my company. For this reason he did not want to part company with me and insisted that I should make my home in Istanbul. But my patriotic sense of duty compelled me to go back to London, to deliver a detailed report concerning the center of the caliphate, and to take new orders.

Throughout my stay in Istanbul I sent reports of my observations monthly to the Ministry of the Commonwealth. I remember asking in one of my reports what I was to do should the person I was working for ask me to practice sodomy with him. The reply was: You can do it if it will help you attain your goal. I was very much indignant over this answer. I felt as if the whole world had fallen down on my head. I already knew that this vicious deed was very common in England. Yet it had never occurred to me that my superiors would command me to commit it. What could I do? I had no other way than to empty the drug to the dregs. So I kept quiet and went on with my duty.

As I said farewell to "Ahmed Efendi", his eyes became wet and he said to me, "My son! May Allâhu ta'âlâ be with you! If you should come back to Istanbul and see that I am dead, remember me. Say the (sûra) **Fâtiha** for my soul! We will meet on the Judgement Day before 'Rasûlullah'." Indeed, I felt very sad, too; so much so that I shed warm tears. However, my sense of duty was naturally stronger.

Chapter III

My friends had returned to London before I did, and they had already received new directives from the Ministry. I, too, was given new directives upon returning. Unfortunately, only six of us were back.

One of the other four people, the secretary said, had become a Muslim and remained in Egypt. Yet the secretary was still pleased because, he said, he (the person who had remained in Egypt) had not betrayed any secrets. The second one had gone to Russia and remained there. He was Russian in origin. The secretary was very sorry about him, not because he had gone back to his homeland, but because perhaps he had been spying on the Ministry of the Commonwealth for Russia and had gone back home because his mission had been over. The third one, as the secretary related, had died of plague in a town named "Imara" in the neighborhood of Baghdâd. The fourth person had been traced by the Ministry up to the city of San'â in the Yemen, and they had received his reports for one year, and, thereafter his reporting had come to an end and no trail of him had been found despite all sorts of efforts. The Ministry put down the disappearance of these four men as a catastrophe. For we are a nation with great duties versus a small population. We therefore do very fine calculations on every man.

After a few of my reports, the secretary held a meeting to scrutinize the reports given by the four of us. When my friends submitted their reports pertaining to their tasks, I, too, submitted my report. They took some notes from my report. The Minister, the secretary, and some of those who attended the meeting praised my work. Nevertheless, I was the third best. The first grade was won by my friend "George Belcoude", and "Henry Fanse" was the second best.

I had doubtlessly been greatly successful in learning Turkish, Arabic, the Qur'ân and the Sharî'at. Yet I had not managed to prepare for the Ministry a report revealing the weak aspects of the Ottoman Empire. After the two-hour meeting, the secretary asked me the reason for my failure. I said, "My essential duty was to learn languages and the Qur'ân and the Sharî'at. I could not spare time for anything in addition. But I shall please you this time if you trust me." The secretary said I was certainly successful but he wished I had won the first grade. (And he went on):

"O Hempher, your next mission comprises these two tasks:

1- To discover Muslims' weak points and the points through which we can enter their bodies and disjoin their limbs. Indeed, this is the way to beat the enemy.

2- The moment you have detected these points and done what I have told you to, [in other words, when you manage to sow discord among Muslims and set them at loggerheads with one another], you will be the most successful agent and earn a medal from the Ministry."

I stayed in London for six months. I married my

paternal first cousin, "Maria Shvay". At that time I was 22 years old, and she was 23. "Maria Shvay was a very pretty girl, with average intelligence and an ordinary cultural background. The happiest and the most cheerful days of my life were those that I spent with her. My wife was pregnant. We were expecting our new guest, when I received the message containing the order that I should leave for Iraq.

Receiving this order at a time while I was awaiting the birth of my son made me sad. However, the importance I attached to my country, compounded with my ambition to attain fame by being chosen the best one among my colleagues, was above my emotions as a husband and as a father. So I accepted the task without hesitation. My wife wanted me to postpone the mission till after the child's birth. Yet I ignored what she said. We were both weeping as we said farewell to each other. My wife said, "Don't stop writing to me! I shall write you letters about our new home, which is as valuable as gold." These words of hers stirred up storms in my heart. I almost cancelled the journey. Yet I managed to take control of my emotions. Extending my farewell to her, I left for the ministry to receive the final instructions.

Six months later I found myself in the city of Basra, Iraq. The city people were partly Sunnite and partly Shiite. Basra was a city of tribes with a mixed population of Arabs, Persians and a relatively small number of Christians. It was the first time in my life that I met with the Persians. By the way, let me touch upon 17 – Shi'ism and Sunnism.

Shiites say that they follow 'Alî bin Abû Tâlib, who was the husband of Muhammad's 'alaihis-salâm' daughter Fâtima and at the same time Muhammad's 'alaihis-salâm' paternal first cousin. They say that Muhammad 'alaihis-salâm' appointed 'Alî and the twelve imâms, 'Alî's descendants to succeed him as the Khalîfa.

In my opinion, the Shi'îs are right in the matter pertaining to the caliphate of 'Alî, Hasan, and Huseyn. For, as far as I understand from the Islamic history, 'Alî was a person with the distinguished and high qualifications required for caliphate. Nor do I find it alien for Muhammad 'alaihis-salâm' to have appointed Hasan and Huseyn as Khalîfas. What makes me suspect, however, is Muhammad's 'alaihis-salâm' having appointed Huseyn's son and eight of his grandsons as Khalîfas. For Huseyn was a child at Muhammad's 'alaihis-salâm' death. How did he know he would have eight grandsons. If Muhammad 'alaihis-salâm' was really a Prophet, it was possible for him to know the future by being informed by Allâhu ta'âlâ, as Jesus Christ had divined about the future. Yet Muhammad's 'alaihis-salâm' prophethood is a matter of doubt to us Christians.

Muslims say that "There are many proofs for Muhammad's 'alaihis-salâm' prophethood. One of them is the Qur'ân (Koran)." I have read the Qur'ân. Indeed, it is a very high book. It is even higher than the Torah (Taurah) and the Bible. For it contains principles, regulations, moral rules, etc.

It has been a wonder to me how an illiterate person

such as Muhammad 'alaihis-salâm' could have brought such a lofty book, and how could he have had all those moral, intellectual and personal qualifications which could not be possessed even by a man who has read and travelled very much. I wonder if these facts were the proofs for Muhammad's 'alaihis-salâm' prophethood?

I always made observations and research in order to elicit the truth about Muhammad's 'alaihis-salâm' prophethood. Once I brought out my interest to a priest in London. His answer was fanatical and obdurate, and was not convincing at all. I asked Ahmed Efendi several times when I was in Turkey, yet I did not receive a satisfactory answer from him, either. To tell the truth, I avoided asking Ahmed Efendi questions directly related to the matter lest they should become suspicious about my espionage.

I think very much of Muhammad 'alaihis-salâm'. No doubt, he is one of Allah's Prophets about whom we have read in books.

Yet, being a Christian, I have not believed in his Prophethood yet. It is doubtless that he was very much superior to geniuses.

The Sunnites, on the other hand, say, "After the Prophet's passing away, Muslims considered Abû Bekr and 'Umar and 'Uthmân and 'Alî suitable for the caliphate."

Controversies of this sort exist in all religions, most abundantly in Christianity. Since both 'Umar and 'Alî are dead today, maintaining these controversies would serve no useful purpose. To me, if Muslims are reasonable, they should think of today, not of those very old days.[3]

One day in the Ministry of the Commonwealth I made a reference to the difference between the Sunnites and the Shiites, saying, "If Muslims knew something about life, they would resolve this Shiite-Sunnite difference among themselves and come together." Someone interrupted me and remonstrated, "Your duty is to provoke this difference, not to think of how to bring Muslims together."

Before I set out for my journey to Iraq, the secretary said, "O Hempher, you should know that there has been natural differences among human beings since God created Abel and Cain. These controversies shall continue until the return of Jesus Christ. So is the case with racial, tribal, territorial, national, and religious controversies.

---

[3] In Shi'îsm it is essential to talk and to have a certain belief on matters concerning the caliphate. According to Sunnî belief these are not necessary. The young Englishman confuses religious information with information pertaining to worldly matters. In worldly knowledge, Muslims have, like he advises, always thought of novelty and improvement, and have always made progress in science, technique, mathematics, architecture, and medicine. When the famous Italian astronomer Galileo said that the earth was rotating – no doubt he had learnt the fact from Muslims – not only was he anathemized by priests, but he was also imprisoned. It was only when he made penance, renouncing his former statement and saying that "No, it is not rotating," that he saved himself from the priests' hands. Muslims follow Qur'ân al-kerîm and hadîth-i-sherîfs in knowledge pertaining to Islam and îmân. Unlike Christians, they do not interpolate this knowledge, which is beyond mind's periphery of activity.

"Your duty this time is to diagnose these controversies well and to report to the ministry. The more successful you are in aggravating the differences among Muslims the greater will be your service to England."

"We, the English people, have to make mischief and arouse schism in all our colonies in order that we may live in welfare and luxury. Only by means of such instigations will we be able to demolish the Ottoman Empire. Otherwise, how could a nation with a small population bring another nation with a greater population under its sway? Look for the mouth of the chasm with all your might, and get in as soon as you find it. You should know that the Ottoman and Iranian Empires have reached the nadir of their existence. Therefore, your first duty is to instigate the people against the administration! History has shown that 'The source of all sorts of revolutions is public rebellions.' When the unity of Muslims is broken and the common sympathy among them is impaired, their forces will be dissolved and thus we shall easily destroy them."

HEMPHER

Chapter IV

When I arrived in Basra, I settled in a mosque. The imâm of the mosque was a Sunnite person of Arabic origin named Shaikh 'Umar Tâî. When I met him I began to chat with him. Yet he suspected me at the very beginning and subjected me to a shower of questions. I managed to survive this dangerous chat as follows: "I am from Turkey's Iğdır region. I was a disciple of Ahmed Efendi of Istanbul. I worked for a carpenter named Khâlid (Hâlid)." I gave him some information about Turkey, which I had acquired during my stay there. Also, I said a few sentences in Turkish. The imâm made an eye signal to one of the people there and asked him if I spoke Turkish correctly. The answer was positive. Having convinced the imâm, I was very happy. Yet I was wrong. For a few days later, I saw to my disappointment that the imâm suspected that I was a Turkish spy. Afterwards, I found out that there was some disagreement and hostility between him and the governor appointed by the (Ottoman) Sultan.

Having been compelled to leave Shaikh 'Umar Efendi's mosque, I rented a room in an inn for travellers and foreigners and moved there. The owner of the inn was an idiot named Murshid Efendi. Every morning he would disturb me by knocking hard at my door to wake me up as soon as the adhân for morning prayer was called. I had to obey him. So, I would get up and perform the morning prayer. Then he would say, "You shall read Qur'ân-al kerîm after morning prayer." When I told him that it was not fard (an act

35

commanded by Islam) to read Qur'ân al- kerîm and asked him why he should insist so much, he would answer, "Sleeping at this time of day will bring poverty and misfortune to the inn and the inmates." I had to carry out this command of his. For he said otherwise he would send me out of the inn. Therefore, as soon as the adhân was called, I would perform morning prayer and then read Qur'ân al-kerîm for one hour.

One day Murshid Efendi came to me and said, "Since you rented this room misfortunes have been befalling me. I put it down to your ominousness. For you are single. Being single (unmarried) portends ill omen. You shall either get married or leave the inn." I told him I did not have property enough to get married. I could not tell him what I had told Ahmed Efendi. For Murshid Efendi was the kind of person who would undress me and examine my genitals to see whether I was telling the truth.

When I said so, Murshid Efendi reproved me, saying, "What a weak belief you have! Haven't you read Allah's âyat purporting, **'If they are poor, Allâhu ta'âlâ will make them rich with His kindness'?[4]**" I was stupefied. At last I said, "All right, I shall get married. But are you ready to provide the necessary money? Or can you find a girl who will cost me little?"

After reflecting for a while, Murshid Efendi said, "I don't care! Either get married by the beginning of Rajab month, or leave the inn." There were only twenty-five days before the beginning of the month of Rajab.

---

[4] Nûr sûra, âyat: 32

Incidentally, let me mention the Arabic months: Muharram, Safar, Rabi'ul-awwal, Rabi'ul-âkhir, Jemâziy-ul-awwal, Jemâziy- ul-âkhir, Rajab, Sha'bân, Ramadân, Shawwâl, Zilqa'da, Zilhijja. Their months are neither more than thirty days, nor below twenty- nine. They are based on lunar calculations.

Taking a job as an assistant to a carpenter, I left Murshid Efendi's inn. We made an agreement on a very low wage, but my lodging and food were to be at the employer's expense. I moved my belongings to the carpenter's shop well before the month of Rajab. The carpenter was a manly person. He treated me as if I were his son. He was a Shiite from Khorasan, Iran, and his name was Abd-ur-Ridâ. Taking the advantage of his company, I began to learn Persian. Every afternoon Iranian Shiites would meet at his place and talk on various subjects from politics to economy. More often than not, they would speak ill of their own government and also of the Khalîfa in Istanbul. Whenever a stranger came in they would change the subject and begin to talk on personal matters.

They trusted me very much. However, as I found out later on, they thought I was an Azerbaijani because I spoke Turkish.

From time to time a young man would call at our carpenter's shop. His attirement was that of a student doing scientific research, and he understood Arabic, Persian, and Turkish. His name was **Muhammad bin Abd-ul-Wahhâb Najdî**. This youngster was an extremely rude and very nervous person. While abusing the Ottoman government very much, he would never speak ill of the Iranian government. The common ground which made him and the shop-owner Abd-ur-Ridâ so friendly was that both were inimical towards the Khalîfa in Istanbul. But how was it possible that this young man, who was a Sunnî, understood Persian and was friends with Abd-ur-Ridâ, who was a Shi'î? In this city Sunnites pretended to be friendly and even brotherly with Shiites. Most of the city's inhabitants understood both Arabic and Persian. And most people understood Turkish as well.

Muhammad of Najd was a Sunnî outwardly. Although most Sunnites censured Shiites, — in fact, they say that Shiites are disbelievers — this man never would revile Shiites. According to Muhammad of Najd, there was no reason for Sunnites to adapt themselves to one of the four madh-habs; he would say, "Allah's Book does not contain any evidence pertaining to these madh- habs." He purposefully ignored the âyet-i-kerîmas on this subject and slighted the hadîth-i-sherîfs.

Concerning the matter of four madh-habs: A century after the death of their Prophet Muhammad 'alaihis-salâm', four scholars came forward from among Sunnite Muslims: Abû Hanîfa, Ahmad bin Hanbal, Mâlik bin Anas, and Muhammad bin Idris Shâfi'î. Some Khalîfas forced the Sunnites to imitate one of these four scholars. They said no one except these four scholars could perform ijtihâd in Qur'ân al-kerîm or with the Sunna. This movement closed the gates of knowledge and understanding for Muslims. This prohibition of ijtihâd is considered to have been the reason for Islam's standstill.

Shiites exploited these erroneous statements to promulgate their sect. The number of Shiites was smaller than one-tenth that of Sunnites. But now they have increased and become equal with Sunnites in number. This result is natural. For ijtihâd is like a weapon. It will improve Islam's fiqh and renovate the understanding of Qur'ân al-kerîm and Sunna. The prohibition of ijtihâd, on the other hand, is like a rotten weapon. It will confine the madh-habs within a certain framework. And this, in its turn, means to close the gates of inference and to disregard the time's requirements. If your weapon is rotten and your enemy is perfect, you are doomed to be beaten by your enemy sooner or later. I think, the clever ones of the Sunnites will reopen the gate of ijtihâd in the future. If they do not do this, they will become the minority, and the Shiites will receive a majority in a few centuries.

[However, the imâms (leaders) of the four madh-habs hold the same creed, the same belief. There is no difference among them. Their difference is only in worships. And this, in turn, is a facility for Muslims. The Shiites, on the other hand, parted into twelve sects, thus becoming a rotten weapon. There is detailed information in this respect in the book **Milal wa Nihal**.]

The arrogant youngster, Muhammad of Najd, would follow his nafs (his sensuous desires) in understanding the Qur'ân and the Sunna. He would completely ignore the views of scholars, not only those of the scholars of his time and the leaders of the four madh-habs, but also those of the notable Sahâbîs such as Abû Bakr and 'Umar. Whenever he came across a Koranic (Qur'ân) verse which he thought was contradictory with the views of those people, he would say, "The Prophet said: **'I have left the Qur'ân and the Sunna for you.'** He did not say, 'I have left the Qur'ân, the Sunna, the Sahâba, and the imâms of madh-habs for you.'[5] Therefore, the thing which is fard is to follow the Qur'ân and the Sunna no matter how contrary they may seem to be to the views of the madh-habs or to the statements of the Sahâba and scholars."[6]

During a dinner conversation at Abd-ur-Ridâ's place, the following dispute took place between Muhammad of Najd and a guest from Kum, a Shiite scholar named Shaikh Jawad:

Shaikh Jawad – Since you accept that 'Alî was a mujtahid, why don't you follow him like Shiites?

Muhammad of Najd – 'Alî is no different from 'Umar or other in a manner to satisfy the time's requirements. Sahâbîs. His statements cannot be of a documentary capacity. Only the Qur'ân and the Sunna are authentic documents. [The fact is that statements

---

[5] This statement of his denies the hadîth-i-sherîf which commands us to follow the Sahâba.

[6] Today in all the Islamic countries ignorant and traitorous people disguised as religious people have been attacking the scholars of Ahl as-sunna. They have been commending Wahhabiism in return for large sums of money they receive from Saudi Arabia. All of them use the abovementioned statements of Muhammad of Najd as a weapon on every occasion. The fact is that none of the statements made by the scholars of Ahl as-sunna or the four imâms is contrary to Qur'ân al- kerîm and hadîth-i-sherîfs. They did not make any additions to these sources, but they explained them. Wahhabis, like their British prototypes, are fabricating lies and misleading Muslims.

made by any of the As-hab-i kiram are of a documentary capacity. Our Prophet commanded us to follow any one of them.[7]

Shaikh Jawâd – Since our Prophet said, **"I am the city of knowledge, and 'Alî is its gate,"** shouldn't there be difference between 'Alî and the other Sahâba?

Muhammad of Najd — If 'Alî's statements were of a documentary capacity, would not the Prophet have said, "I have left you the Qur'ân, the Sunna, and 'Alî"?

Shaikh Jawâd — Yes, we can assume that he (the Prophet) said so. For he stated in a hadîth-i-sherîf, **"I leave** (behind me) **Allah's Book and my Ahl-i-Bayt."** And 'Alî, in his turn, is the greatest member of the Ahl-i-Bayt.

Muhammad of Najd denied that the Prophet had said so.

Shaikh Jawâd confuted Muhammad of Najd with convincing proofs.

However, Muhammad of Najd objected to this and said, "You assert that the Prophet said, **'I leave you Allah's Book and my Ahl- i-Bayt.'** Then, what has become of the Prophet's Sunna?"

Shaikh Jawâd — The Sunna of the Messenger of Allah is the explanation of the Qur'ân. The Messenger

---

[7] A Muslim who has seen the beautiful, blessed face of Muhammad 'alaihis-salâm' is called Sahâbî. Plural for Sahâbî is Sahâba, or As- hâb.

of Allah said, **"I leave** (you) **Allah's Book and my Ahl-i-Bayt."** The phrase 'Allah's Book' includes the 'Sunna', which is an explanation of the former.

Muhammad of Najd — Inasmuch as the statements of the Ahl- i-Bayt are the explanations of the Qur'ân, why should it be necessary to explain it by hadîths?

Shaikh Jawâd — When hadrat Prophet passed away, his Ummat (Muslims) considered that there should be an explanation of the Qur'ân which would satisfy the time's requirements. It was for this reason that hadrat Prophet commanded his Ummat to follow the Qur'ân, which is the original, and his Ahl-i-Bayt, who were to explain the Qur'ân.

I liked this dispute very much. Muhammad of Najd was motionless in front of Shaikh Jawâd, like a house-sparrow in the hands of a hunter.

Muhammad of Najd was the sort I had been looking for. For his scorn for the time's scholars, his slighting even the (earliest) four Khalîfas, his having an independent view in understanding the Qur'ân and the Sunna were his most vulnerable points to hunt and obtain him. So different this conceited youngster was from that Ahmed Efendi who had taught me in Istanbul! That scholar, like his predecessors, was reminiscent of a mountain. No power would be able to move him. Whenever he mentioned the name of Abû Hanîfa, he would stand up, go and make an ablution. Whenever he meant to hold the book of Hadîth named **Bukhârî,** he would, again, make an ablution. The Sunnîs trust this book very much.

Muhammed of Najd, on the other hand, disdained Abû Hanîfa very much. He would say, "I know better than Abû Hanîfa did.[8]" In addition, according to him, half of the book of **Bukhârî** was wrong.[9]

[As I was translating these confessions of Hempher's into Turkish,[10] I remembered the following event: I was a teacher in a high school. During a lesson one of my students asked, "Sir, if a Muslim is killed in a war, will he become a martyr?" "Yes, he will," I said. "Did the Prophet say so?" "Yes, he did." "Will he become a martyr if he is drowned in sea, too?" "Yes," was my answer. "And in this case he will attain more thawâb." Then he asked, "Will he become a martyr if he falls down from an aeroplane?" "Yes, he will," I said. "Did our Prophet state these, too?" "Yes, he did." Upon this, he smiled in a triumphant air and said, "Sir! Were there aeroplanes in those days?" My answer to him was as follows: "My son! Our Prophet has ninety-nine names. Each of his names stands for a beautiful attribute he was endowed with. One of his names is **Jâmi'ul-kalim.** He would state many facts in one word. For example, he said, **'He who falls from a height will become a martyr.'** " The child admitted this answer of mine with admiration and gratitude. By the same token, Qur'ân al-kerîm and hadîth-i-sherîfs contain many words, rules,

---

[8] Some ignorant people without a certain madh-hab today, say so, too.

[9] This allegation of this person shows that he was quite unaware of the knowledge of Hadîth.

[10] Hempher's confessions were translated into Turkish and, together with the author's explanations, formed a book. This version is the Eglish translation of that Turkish book.

commandments and prohibitions each of which denotes various other meanings. The scientific work carried on to explore these meanings and to apply the right ones to the right cases, is called **Ijtihâd.** Performing ijtihâd requires having profound knowledge. For this reason, the Sunnîs prohibited ignorant people from attempting ijtihâd. This does not mean to prohibit ijtihâd. After the fourth century of the Hegiral Era, no scholars were educated so highly as to reach the grade of an absolute mujtahid [scholar profoundly learned (enough to perform ijtihâd)]; therefore, no one performed ijtihad, which in turn naturally meant the closure of the gates of ijtihâd. Towards the end of the world, Îsâ (Jesus) 'alaihis-salâm' shall descend from heaven and Mahdî (the expected Islamic hero) shall appear; these people shall perform ijtihâd.

Our Prophet 'sall-Allâhu alaihi wa sallam' stated, **"After me Muslims shall part into seventy-three groups. Only one of these groups shall enter Paradise."** When he was asked who were to be in that group, he answered, **"Those who adapt themselves to me and my As-hâb."** In another hadîth-i-sherîf he stated, **"My Ashâb are like celestial stars. You will attain hidâyat if you follow any one of them!"** In other words, he said, "You will attain the way leading to Paradise." A Jew of Yemen, Abdullah bin Saba' by name, instigated hostility against the As-hâb among Muslims. Those ignorant people who believed this Jew and bore enmity against the As-hâb were called **Shi'î** (Shiite). And people who obeyed the hadîth-sherîfs, loved and followed the As-hâb-i-kirâm were called **Sunnî** (Sunnite).]

I established a very intimate friendship with Muhammad bin Abd-ul-Wahhâb of Najd. I launched a campaign of praising him everywhere. One day I said to him: "You are greater than 'Umar and 'Alî. If the Prophet were alive now, he would appoint you as his Khalîfa instead of them. I expect that Islam will be renovated and improved in your hands. You are the only scholar who will spread Islam all over the world."

Muhammad the son of Abd-ul-Wahhâb and I decided to make a new interpretation of the Qur'ân; this new interpretation was to reflect only our points of view and would be entirely contrary to those explanations made by the Sahâba, by the imâms of madh- habs and by the mufassirs (deeply learned scholars specialized in the explanation of the Qur'ân). We were reading the Qur'ân and talking on some of the âyats. My purpose in doing this was to mislead Muhammad. After all, he was trying to present himself as a revolutionist and would therefore accept my views and ideas with pleasure so that I should trust him all the more.

On one occasion I said to him, "Jihâd (fighting, struggling for Islam) is not fard."

He protested, "Why shouldn't it be despite Allah's commandment, **'Make war against unbelievers.'?**"[11]

I said, "Then why didn't the Prophet make war against the munâfiqs despite Allah's commandment,

---

[11] Tawba sûra, âyat: 73

'Make Jihâd against unbelievers and munâfiqs.'?"[12]
[On the other hand, it is written in **Mawâhibu ladunniyya** that twenty-seven Jihâds were performed against unbelievers. Their swords are exhibited in Istanbul's museums. Munâfiqs would pretend to be Muslims. They would perform namâz with the Messenger of Allah in the Masjîd-i- Nabawî during the days. Rasûlullah 'sall-Allâhu alaihi wasallam' knew them. Yet he did not say, " You are a munâfiq," to any of them. If he had made war against them and killed them, people would say, "Muhammad 'alaihis-salâm' killed people who believed in him." Therefore he made verbal Jihâd against them. For Jihâd, which is fard, is performed with one's body and/or with one's property and/or with one's speech. The âyat-i-kerîma quoted above commands to perform Jihâd against unbelievers. It does not define the type of the Jihâd to be performed. For Jihâd against unbelievers must be performed by fighting, and Jihâd against munâfiqs is to be performed by preaching and advice. This âyat-i-kerîma covers these types of Jihâd.]

He said, "The Prophet made Jihâd against them with his speech."

I said, "Is the Jihâd which is fard (commanded), the one which is to be done with one's speech?"

He said, "Rasûlullah made war against the unbelievers."

I said, "The Prophet made war against the

---

[12] Tawba sûra, âyat: 73

unbelievers in order to defend himself. For the
unbelievers intended to kill him."

He nodded.

At another time I said to him, "Mut'a nikâh[13] is
permissible."

He objected, "No, it is not."

I said, "Allah declares, **'In return for the use you
make of them, give them the mehr you have
decided upon'.**[14]

He said, "'Umar prohibited two examples of mut'a
practice existent in his time and said he would punish
anyone who practiced it."

I said, "You both say that you are superior to 'Umar
and follow him. In addition, 'Umar said he prohibited it
though he knew that the Prophet had permitted it.[15]

---

[13] Nikâh means a marriage contract as prescribed by Islam. Mut'a nikâh
means a contract made between a man and a woman to cohabit for a
certain period of time. Islam prohibits this type of marriage.

[14] Nisâ sûra, âyat: 24

[15] Mut'a nikâh is similar to today's practice of having a mistress. It is
permissible according to the Shiites. 'Umar 'radiy-Allâhu anh' did not say
so. Like all other Christians, the English spy bears hostility towards hadrat
'Umar and inveighs against him on this occasion, too. It is written in the
book **Hujaj-i-Qat'iyya:** "'Umar 'radiy-Allâhu anh' said that Rasûlullah
had forbidden mut'a nikâh and that he was not going to permit a practice
forbidden by the Messenger of Allah. All the As-hâb-i-kirâm supported
this statement of the Khalîfa's. Among them was hadrat Alî, too." (Please
see the book **Documents of the Right Word.**)

Why do you leave aside the Prophet's word and obey 'Umar's word?"

He did not answer. I knew that he was convinced.

I sensed that Muhammad of Najd desired a woman at that moment; he was single. I said to him, "Come on, let us each get a woman by mut'a nikâh. We will have a good time with them. He accepted with a nod. This was a great opportunity for me, so I promised to find a woman for him to amuse himself. My aim was to allay the timidity he had about people. But he stated it a condition that the matter be kept as a secret between us and that the woman not even be told what his name was. I hurriedly went to the Christian women who had been sent forth by the Ministry of the Commonwealth with the task of seducing the Muslim youth there. I explained the matter to one of them. She accepted to help, so I gave her the nickname Safiyya. I took Muhammad of Najd to her house. Safiyya was at home, alone. We made a one-week marriage contract for Muhammad of Najd, who gave the woman some gold in the name of **Mehr.** Thus we began to mislead Muhammad of Najd, Safiyya from within, and I from without.

Muhammad of Najd was thoroughly in Safiyya's hands now. Besides, he had tasted the pleasure of disobeying the commandments of the Sharî'at under the pretext of freedom of ijtihâd and ideas.

The third day of the mut'a nikâh I had a long dispute with him over that hard drinks were not harâm (forbidden by Islam). Although he quoted many âyats and hadîths showing that it was harâm to have hard drinks, I cancelled all of them and finally said, "It is a fact that Yezîd and the Umayyad and Abbasid Khalîfas had hard drinks. Were they all miscreant people and you are the only adherent of the right way? They doubtless knew the Qur'ân and the Sunna better than you do. They inferred from the Qur'ân and the Sunna that the hard drink is makrûh, not harâm. Also, it is written in Jewish and Christian books that alcohol is mubâh (permitted). All religions are Allah's commandments. In fact, according to a narrative, 'Umar had hard drinks until the revelation of the âyat, **'You have all given it up, haven't you?"**[16] If it had been harâm, the Prophet would have chastised him. Since the Prophet did not punish him, hard drink is halâl." [The fact is that 'Umar 'radiy- Allâhu anh' used to take hard drinks before they were made harâm. He never drank after the prohibition was declared. If some of the Umayyad and Abbasid Khalîfas took alcoholic drinks, this would not show that drinks with alcohol are makrûh. It would show that they were sinners, that they committed harâm. For the âyat-i- kerîma quoted by the spy, as well as other âyat-i-kerîmas and hadîth-i-sherîfs, shows that drinks with alcohol are harâm. It is stated in **Riyâd-un-nâsihîn,** "Formerly it was permissible to drink wine. Hadrat 'Umar, Sa'd ibni Waqqas, and some other Sahâbîs used to drink wine. Later the two hundred and nineteenth âyat of Baqara sûra was revealed to declare that it was a grave sin. Sometime later the forty-second âyat of Nisâ sûra was revealed and it was declared, **"Do not approach the namâz when you are drunk!"** Eventually, the ninety-third

---

[16] Mâida sûra, âyat: 91

âyat of Mâida sûra came and wine was made harâm. It was stated as follows in hadîth-i-sherîfs: **"If something would intoxicate in case it were taken in a large amount, it is harâm to take it even in a small amount."** and **"Wine is the gravest of sins."** and **"Do not make friends with a person who drinks wine! Do not attend his funeral** (when he dies)**! Do not form a matrimonial relationship with him!"** and **"Drinking wine is like worshipping idols."** and **"May Allâhu ta'âlâ curse him who drinks wine, sells it, makes it, or gives it."**]

Muhammad of Najd said, "According to some narratives, 'Umar drank alcoholic spirits after mixing it with water and said it was not harâm unless it had an intoxicating effect. 'Umar's view is correct, for it is declared in the Qur'ân, **'The devil wants to stir up enmity and grudge among you and to keep you from doing dhikr of Allah and from namâz by means of drinks and gambling. You will give these up now, won't you?"**[17] Alcoholic spirits will not cause the sins defined in the âyat when they do not intoxicate. Therefore, hard drinks are not harâm when they don't have an intoxicating effect."[18]

I told Safiyya about this dispute we had on drinks and instructed her to make him drink a very strong spirit. Afterwards, she said, "I did as you said and made him drink. He danced and united with me several times

---

[17] Mâida sûra, âyat: 91

[18] However, our Prophet stated, "If something would intoxicate in case it were taken in a large amount, it is harâm to take even a small amount of it which would not intoxicate."

that night." From then on Safiyya and I completely took control of Muhammad of Najd. In our farewell talk the Minister of the Commonwealth had said to me, "We captured Spain from the disbelievers [he means Muslims] by means of alcohol and fornication. Let us take all our lands back by using these two great forces again." Now I know how true a statement it was.

One day I broached the topic of fasting to Muhammad of Najd: "It is stated in the Qur'ân, **'Your fasting is more auspicious for you.'**[19] It is not stated that fasting is fard (a plain commandment). Then, fasting is sunna, not fard, in the Islamic religion." He protested and said, "Are you trying to lead me out of my faith?" I replied, "One's faith consists of the purity of one's heart, the salvation of one's soul, and not committing a transgression against others' rights. Did not the Prophet state, **'Faith is love'?** Did not Allah declare in Qur'ân al-kerîm, **'Worship thine Rabb (Allah) until yaqîn**[20] **comes to thee'?**[21] Then, when one has attained yaqîn pertaining to Allah and the Day of Judgement and beautified one's heart and purified one's deeds, one will become the most virtuous of mankind." He shook his head in reply to these words of mine.

Once I said to him, "Namâz is not fard." "How is it not fard?"

---

[19]. Baqara sûra, âyat: 184

[20] All the Islamic books agree that (Yaqîn) in this context means (death) Hence this âyat-i-kerîma purports, **"Worship till death."**

[21] Hijr Sûra, âyat: 99

51

"Allah declares in the Qur'ân, **'Perform namâz to remember Me.'**[22] Then, the aim of namâz is to remember Allah. Therefore, you might as well remember Allah without performing namâz."

He said, "Yes. I have heard that some people do dhikr of Allah instead of performing namâz."[23] I was very much pleased with this statement of his. I tried hard to develop this notion and capture his heart. Then I noticed that he did not attach much importance to namâz and was performing it quite sporadically. He was very negligent especially with the morning prayer. For I would keep him from going to bed by talking with him until midnight. So he would be too exhausted to get up for morning prayer.

I began to pull down the shawl of belief slowly off the shoulders of Muhammad of Najd. One day I wanted to dispute with him about the Prophet, too. "From now on, if you talk with me on these topics, our relation will be spoilt and I shall put an end to my friendship with you." Upon this I gave up speaking about the Prophet for fear of ruining all my endeavours once and for all.

I advised him to pursue a course quite different from those of Sunnites and Shiites. He favoured this idea of

---

[22] Tâhâ sûra, âyat: 14

[23] Our Prophet stated, "The namâz is Islam's pillar. He who performs namâz has constructed his faith. He who does not (perform namâz) has ruined his faith;" and (in another hadîth), "Perform namâz as I do." It is a grave sin not to perform namâz in this manner. What signifies the heart's purity is to perform namâz correctly.

mine. For he was a conceited person. Thanks to Safiyya, I put an halter on him.

On one occasion I said, "I have heard that the Prophet made his As-hâb brothers to one another. Is it true?" Upon his positive reply, I wanted to know if this Islamic rule was temporary or permanent. He explained, "It is permanent. For the Prophet Muhammad's halâl is halâl till the end of the world, and his harâm is harâm till the end of the world." Then I offered him to be my brother. So we were brothers.

From that day on I never left him alone. We were together even in his travels. He was very important for me. For the tree that I had planted and grown, spending the most valuable days of my youth, was now beginning to yield its fruit.

I was sending monthly reports to the Ministry of the Commonwealth in London. The answers I received were very encouraging and reassuring. Muhammad of Najd was following the path I had drawn for him.

My duty was to imbue him with feelings of independence, freedom and scepticism. I always praised him, saying that a brilliant future was awaiting him.

One day I fabricated the following dream: "Last night I dreamed of our Prophet. I addressed him with the attributes I had learnt from hodjas. He was seated on a dais. Around him were scholars that I did not know. You entered. Your face was as bright as haloes. You walked towards the Prophet, and when you were close enough the Prophet stood up and kissed between your both eyes. He said, 'You are my namesake, the heir to my knowledge, my deputy in worldly and religious matters.' You said, 'O Messenger of Allah! I am afraid to explain my knowledge to people.' 'You are the greatest. Don't be afraid,' replied the Prophet.''

Muhammad bin Abd-ul-Wahhâb was wild with joy when he heard the dream. He asked several times if what I had told him was true, and received a positive answer each time he asked. Finally he was sure I had told him the truth. I think, from then on, he was resolved to publicise the ideas I had imbued him with and to establish a new sect.[24]

---

[24] The book Al-fajr-us-sâdiq, written by Jamil Sidqi Zahâwî Efendi of Baghdâd, who was a muderris (professor) of Aqâid-i-Islâmiyya (Islamic creed) in the Dâr-ul-funûn (university) of Istanbul and passed away in 1354 [C.E. 1936], was printed in Egypt in 1323 [C.E. 1905] and reproduced by offset process by Hakikat Kitâbevi in Istanbul. It is stated in the book, "The heretical ideas of the Wahhabi sect were produced by Muhammad bin Abd-ul-Wahhâb in Najd in 1143 [C.E. 1730]. He was born in 1111 [C.E. 1699], and died in 1207 [C.E. 1792]. The sect was spread at the cost of a considerable amount of Muslim blood by Muhammad bin Su'ûd, the Emîr of Der'iyya. Wahhabis called Muslims who would not agree with them polytheists. They said that all of them (non-Wahhabis) must perform the hajj anew (even if they had performed it), and asserted that all their ancestors as well had been disbelievers for six hundred years. They killed anyone who would not accept the Wahhabi sect, and carried off their possessions as booties. They imputed ugly motives to Muhammad 'alaihis-salâm'. They burned books of Fiqh, Tafsîr, and Hadîth. They misinterpreted Qur'ân al-kerîm in accordance with their own ideas. In order to deceive Muslims, they said they were in the Hanbalî madh-hab. However, most Hanbalî scholars wrote books refuting them and explaining that they were heretics. They are disbelievers because they call harâms 'halâl' and because they belittle Prophets and the Awliyâ. The Wahhabi religion is based on ten essentials: Allah is a material being. He has hands, a face, and directions. [This belief of theirs is similar to the Christian creed (Father, Son, and Holy Ghots)]; 2- They interpret Qur'ân al-kerîm according to their own understanding; 3- They reject the facts reported by the As-hâb-i-kirâm; 4- They reject the facts reported by

Chapter V

It was on one of those days when Muhammad of Najd and I had become very intimate friends that I received a message from London ordering me to leave for the cities of **Kerbelâ** and **Najaf,** the two most popular Shiite centers of knowledge and spirituality. So I had to put an end to my company with Muhammad of Najd and leave Basra. Yet I was happy because I was sure that this ignorant and morally depraved man was going to establish a new sect, which in turn would demolish Islam from within, and that I was the composer of the heretical tenets of this new sect.

'Alî, the fourth Khalîfa of the Sunnites, and the first one according to the Shiites, was buried in Najaf. The city of **Kûfa,** which was a distance of one fersah (league), i.e., an hour's walk from Najaf, was the capital

---

scholars; 5- They say a person who imitates one of the four madh-habs is a disbeliever; 6- They say non-Wahhabis are disbelievers; 7- They say a person who prays by making the Prophet and the Awliyâ intermediaries (between himself and Allâhu ta'âlâ), will become a disbeliever; 8- They say it is harâm to visit the Prophet's grave or those of the Awliyâ; 9- He who swears on any being other than Allah will become a polytheist, they say; 10- A person who makes a solemn pledge to anyone except Allah or who kills an animal (as a sacrifice) by the graves of Awliyâ, will become a polytheist, they say. In this book of mine it will be proved by documentary evidences that all these ten credal tenets are wrong." These ten fundamentals of the Wahhabi religion are noticeably identical with the religious principles Hempher prompted to Muhammad of Najd.

The British published Hempher's confessions as a means for Christian propaganda. In order to mislead Muslims' children they wrote lies and fabrications in the name of Islamic teachings. Therefore, with a view to protecting our youth from this British trap, we publish this book, which is a correction of their lies and slanders.

of 'Alî's caliphate. When 'Alî was killed, his sons Hasan and Huseyn buried him outside Kûfa at a place called Najaf today. In the course of time, Najaf began to grow, while Kûfa gradually fell into decay. The Shiite men of religion came together in Najaf. Houses, markets, madrasas (Islamic schools and universities) were built.

The Khalîfa in Istanbul was kind and generous to them for the following reasons:

1- The Shiite administration in Iran was supporting the Shiites. The Khalîfa's interfering with them would cause tension between the states, which in turn could lead to warfare.

2- The inhabitants of Najaf included a number of armed tribes supporting the Shiites. Although they did not have much significance in terms of weaponry and organization, it would be unwise for the Khalîfa to run the risk of getting into trouble with them.

3- The Shiites in Najaf had authority over the Shiites all over the world, particularly those in Africa and India. If the Khalîfa disturbed them, all the Shiites would rise against him.

Huseyn bin 'Alî, the Prophet's grandson, i.e., his daughter Fâtima's son, was martyred in Kerbelâ. The people of Iraq had sent for Huseyn in Medina and invited him to Iraq to elect him their Khalîfa. Huseyn and his family were in the territory called Kerbelâ when the Iraqis gave up their former intention and, acting upon the order given by Yazîd bin Muâwiya, the Umayyad Khalîfa living in Damascus, set out with the intention of arresting him. Huseyn and his family put up a heroic last-ditch fight against the Iraqi army. The battle ended in their death, so the Iraqi army was the winning side. Since that day, the Shiites have accepted Kerbelâ as their spiritual center, so that Shiites from all over the world come here and form such a huge crowd that our religion of Christianity does not have a likeness to it.

Kerbelâ, a Shiite city, contains Shiite madrasas. This city and Najaf support each other. Upon receiving the order to go to these two cities, I left Basra for Baghdad, and thence to a city named 'Hulla' situated alongside the Euphrates.

The Tigris and Euphrates come from Turkey, cut through Iraq, and flow into the Persian Gulf. Iraq's agriculture and welfare are due to these two rivers.

When I was back in London, I proposed to the Ministry of the Commonwealth that a project could be drawn up to change the beds of these two rivers in order to make Iraq accept our proposals. When the water was cut off, Iraq would have to satisfy our demands.

From Hulla to Najaf I travelled in the guise of an Azerbaijani tradesman. Establishing close friendships with Shiite men of religion, I began to mislead them. I joined their circles of religious instruction. I saw that they did not study science like the Sunnites, nor did they have the beautiful moral qualities possessed by the Sunnites. For example:

1- They were extremely inimical towards the Porte. For they were Shiites and the Turks were Sunnites.

They said that the Sunnites were disbelievers.

2- The Shiite scholars were entirely absorbed in religious teachings and had very little interest in worldly knowledge, as was the case with priests during the period of standstill in our history.

3- They were quite unaware of Islam's inner essence and sublime character, nor did they have the smallest notion of the time's scientific and technical improvements.

I said to myself: What a wretched sort of people these Shiites are. They are sound asleep when the whole world is awake. One day a flood will come and take them all away. Several times I attempted to entice them to revolt against the Khalîfa. Unfortunately, no one would even listen to me. Some of them laughed at me as though I had told them to destroy the earth. For they looked on the Khalîfa as a fortress impossible to capture. According to them, they would get rid of the caliphate with the advent of the promised Mahdi.

According to them, Mahdi was their twelfth imâm, who was a descendant of Islam's Prophet and who disappeared in the Hijrî year 255. They believed he was still alive and would one day reappear and rescue the world from this state of utter cruelty and injustice, filling it with justice.

It is consternating! How come these Shiite people believe in these superstitions! It was like the superstitious doctrine, "Jesus Christ will come back and fill the world with justice," held by our Christians.

One day I said to one of them: "Isn't it fard for you

to prevent injustice like the Islamic Prophet did?" His reply was: "He managed to prevent injustice because Allah helped him." When I said, "It is written in the Qur'ân, **'If you help Allah's religion, He will help you in return.'**[25] " If you revolt against the torture of your shâhs, Allah will help you" He answered, "You are a tradesman. These are scientific matters. You cannot understand this."

The mausoleum of 'Alî the Emîr-ul-mu'minîn was profusely decorated. It had a splendid yard, a gold-covered dome, and two tall minarets. Every day great numbers of Shiites visited this mausoleum. They performed namâz in jamâ'at in it. Every visitor first stooped in front of the threshold, kissed it, and then greeted the grave. They asked for permission and then entered. The mausoleum had a vast yard, which contained numerous rooms for men of religion and visitors.

There were two mausoleums similar to that of 'Alî's in Kerbelâ. One of them belonged to Huseyn and the other one belonged to his brother **Abbâs,** who had been martyred with him in Kerbelâ. In Kerbelâ the Shiites repeated the same practices as they did in Najaf. The climate of Kerbelâ was better than that of Najaf. It was surrounded with graceful orchards and lovely brooks.

During my mission to Iraq I met with a scene that

---

[25] Muhammad sûra, âyat: 7. To help the religion of Allâhu ta'âlâ means to adapt oneself to the Sharî'at and to try to promulgate it. To revolt against the Shâh or the State would mean to destroy the religion.

gave relief to my heart. Some events heralded the end of the Ottoman Empire. For one thing, the governor appointed by the administration in Istanbul was an uneducated and cruel person. He acted as he wished. The people did not like him. The Sunnites were uneasy because the governor restricted their freedom and did not value them, and the Shiites felt indignant over being governed by a Turk while among them there were sayyids[26] and sherîfs,[27] the Prophet's descendants, who would have been a much better choice for governorship.

The Shiites were in an utterly sorrowful situation. They lived in squalid and dilapidated environments. The roads were not safe. Highwaymen always awaited caravans, and attacked whenever they saw that there were no soldiers escorting them. For this reason, convoys would not set out unless the government would appoint a detachment to escort them.

The Shiite tribes were mostly warlike with one another. They killed and plundered one another daily. Ignorance and illiteracy were dreadfully widespread. This state of the Shiites reminded me of the time when Europe had been under an ecclesiastical invasion. With the exclusion of the religious leaders living in Najaf and Kerbelâ and a small minority, who were their votaries, not even one out of every thousand Shiites knew how to read or write.

---

[26] Descendants of hadrat Huseyn 'radiy-Allâhu anh'.

[27] Descendants of hadrat Hasan 'radiy-Allâhu anh'.

The economy had collapsed entirely, and the people were suffering utter poverty. The administrative system was quite out of order. The Shiites committed treasons against the government.

The State and the people viewed each other with suspicion. As a result, there was no mutual aid between them. The Shiite religious leaders, totally given to vituperating the Sunnites, had already relinquished knowledge; business, religious and worldly alike.

I stayed in Kerbelâ and in Najaf for four months. I suffered a very serious illness in Najaf. I felt so bad that I completely gave up hope of recovery. My illness lasted three weeks. I went to a doctor. He gave me a prescription. Using the medicine, I began to recover. Throughout my illness I stayed in an underground room.

Because I was ill, my host prepared my medicine and food in return for an insignificant sum of money and expected great thawâb for serving me. For I was, so to speak, a visitor of 'Alî the Emîr-ul-mu'minîn. The doctor advised me to have only chicken broth during the first few days. Later on he permitted me to eat chicken as well. The third week I had rice soup. After becoming well again I left for Baghdad. I prepared a report of one hundred pages on my observations in Najaf, Hulla, and Baghdad and while on the way. I submitted the report to the Baghdad representative of the Ministry of the Commonwealth. I waited for the Ministry's order on whether I should remain in Iraq or return to London.

I wished to go back to London. For I had been abroad for a long time. I missed my homeland and my family. Especially, I wanted to see my son Rasputin, who had been born after my departure. For this reason, I appended to my report a petition for permission to return to London for a short time at least. I wanted to give an oral report of impressions about my three-year mission in Iraq and to get some rest in the meantime.

The Iraq representative of the Ministry advised me not to call on him often lest I should arouse suspicion. He also advised to rent a room in one of the inns alongide the Tigris River, and said, "I shall inform you of the Ministry's answer when we receive the mail from London." During my stay in Baghdad I observed the spiritual distance between Istanbul, the capital of the caliphate, and Baghdad.

When I left Basra for Kerbelâ and Najaf, I was very much anxious that Muhammad of Najd would swerve from the direction I had led him. For he was an extremely unstable and nervous person. I feared that the aims I had built upon him might be spoilt.

As I left him he was thinking of going to Istanbul. I did my best to dissuade him from the notion. I said, "I am very anxious that when you go there you may make a statement whereby they will pronounce you a heretic and kill you."

My apprehension was quite the other way round. I was anxious that upon going there he should meet profound scholars capable of setting his fallacies right and converting him to the Sunnî creed and thus all my dreams should come to naught. For there was knowledge and Islam's beautiful morality in Istanbul.

When I found out that Muhammad of Najd did not want to stay in Basra, I recommended that he go to Isfahan and Shîrâz.

For these two cities were lovely. And their inhabitants were Shiites. And Shiites, in their turn, could not possibly influence Muhammad of Najd. For Shiites were inefficient in knowledge and ethics. Thus I made it certain that he would not change the course I had charted for him.

As we parted I said to him, "Do you believe in Taqiyya?" "Yes, I do," he replied. "The unbelievers arrested one of the Sahâba and tormented him and killed his parents. Upon this he made **Taqiyya,** that is, he said openly that he was a polytheist. (When he came back and said what had happened), the Prophet did not reproach him at all." I advised him, "When you live among the Shiites, make Taqiyya; do not tell them that you are Sunnî lest they become a nuisance for you. Utilize their country and scholars! Learn their customs and traditions. For they are ignorant and stubborn people."

As I left, I gave him some money as zakât. Zakât is an Islamic tax collected in order to be dealt out to the needy people. In addition, I gave him a saddled animal as a present. So we parted.

After my departure I lost contact with him. This made me utterly uneasy. When we parted we decided that both of us were to return to Basra and whichever party was back first and did not find the other party was to write a letter and leave it with Abd-ur- Rîdâ.

Chapter VI

I stayed in Baghdad for a time. Then, receiving the message ordering me to return to London, I left. In London, I talked with the secretary and some officials of the Ministry. I told them of my activities and observations during my long mission. They rejoiced greatly at the information I gave about Iraq and said that they were pleased. On the other hand, Safiyya, the girlfriend of Muhammad of Najd, sent a report agreeing with mine. I found out also that throughout my mission I had been followed by men from the Ministry. These men also sent reports concurrent with the reports I had sent and with the account I had given to the secretary.

The secretary made an appointment for me to meet the Minister. When I visited the Minister, he met me in a manner that he had not shown towards me upon my arrival from Istanbul. I knew that I occupied an exceptional place in his heart now.

The minister was very pleased to know that I had obtained Muhammad of Najd. "He is a weapon our Ministry has been looking for. Give him all sorts of promises. It would be worthwhile if you spent all your time indoctrinating him," he said.

When I said, "I have been anxious about Muhammad of Najd. He may have changed his mind," he replied, "Don't worry. He has not given up the ideas he had when you left him. The spies of our Ministry met him in Isfahan and reported to our Ministry that he had not changed." I said to myself, "How could Muhammad of Najd reveal his secrets to a stranger?" I did not dare to ask this question to the Minister. However, when I met Muhammad of Najd later, I found out that in Isfahan a man named Abd-ul-kerîm had met him and ferreted out his secrets by saying, "I am Shaikh Muhammad's [meaning me] brother. He told me all that he knew about you."

Muhammad of Najd said to me, "Safiyya went with me to Isfahan and we cohabited with mut'a nikâh for two more months.

Abd-ul-kerîm accompanied me to Shîrâz and found me a woman named Âsiya, who was prettier and more attractive than Safiyya. Making mut'a nikâh with that woman, I spent the most delightful moments of my life with her."

I found out later that Abd-ul-kerîm was a Christian agent living in the Jelfa district of Isfahan and working for the Ministry. And Âsiya, a Jewess living in Shîrâz, was another agent for the Ministry. All four of us coordinated to train Muhammad of Najd in such a way that in future he would do what was expected from him in the best way.

When I related the events in the presence of the Minister, the secretary, and two other members of the Ministry whom I did not know, the Minister said to me, "You have deserved to receive the greatest award of the Ministry. For you are the best one among the most significant agents of the ministry. The secretary will tell you some State secrets, which will help you in your mission."

Then they gave me a ten-day leave during which I could see my family. So I went home right away and spent some of my sweetest moments with my son, who resembled me very much. My son spoke a few words, and walked so elegantly that I felt as if he were a piece from my own body. I spent this ten-day leave so cheerfully, so happily. I felt as if I were going to fly from joy. It was such a great pleasure to be back home, to be with my family. During this ten-day leave I visited my old paternal aunt, who loved me very much. It was wise of me to visit my paternal aunt. For she passed away after my departure for my third mission. I felt so sad about her decease.

This ten-day leave elapsed as fast as an hour. Whereas cheerful days such as these go by as quickly as an hour, days of grief seem to take centuries. I remembered the days when I had suffered that illness in Najaf. Those days of affliction had seemed like years to me.

When I went to the Ministry to receive new orders, I met the secretary with his cheerful face and tall stature. He shook my hand so warmly that his affection was perceptible.

He said to me, "With the command of our minister and the committee in charge of Colonies, I shall tell you two State secrets. Later you will benefit very much from these two secrets. No one except a couple of confidential people know these two secrets."

Holding my hand, he took me to a room in the Ministry. I met with something very attractive in this room. Ten men were sitting around a round table. The first man was in the guise of the Ottoman Emperor. He spoke Turkish and English. The second one was dressed in the attire of the Shaikh-ul-islâm (Chief of Islamic Matters) in Istanbul. The third one was dressed in an attirement identical with that of the Shah of Iran. The fourth one was in the atttire of the vizier in the Iranian palace. The fifth one was dressed like the great scholar leading the Shiites in Najaf. The last three of these people spoke Persian and English. Each of these five people had a clerk sitting beside him to write down whatever they would say. These clerks were imparting to the five men the information collected by spies about their archetypes in Istanbul, Iran, and Najaf.

The secretary said, "These five people represent the five people there. In order to know what their archetypes think, we have educated and trained these people exactly like their archetypes. We intimate the information we have obtained about their originals in Istanbul, Teheran and Najaf to these men. And these men, in their turn, imagine themselves to be their originals in those places. Then we ask them and they answer us. We have determined that the answers given by these people are seventy- percent agreeable with the answers that their originals would give.

"If you like, you may ask questions for assessment. You have already met the scholar of Najaf." I replied in the affirmative, for I had met the great Shiite scholar in Najaf and asked him about some matters. Now I approached his copy and said, "Dear teacher, would it be permissible for us to wage war against the government because it is Sunnî and fanatical?" He reflected for a while, and said, "No, it is not permissible for us to wage war against the government because it is Sunnî. For all Muslims are brothers. We could declare war on them (Sunnite Muslims) only if they perpetrated cruelty and persecution on the Ummat (Muslims). And even in this case we would observe the principles of Amr-i-bi- l-ma'rûf[28] and Nahy-i-ani-l-munkar.[29] We would stop interfering with them as soon as they stopped their persecution."

I said, "Dear teacher, may I have your opinion concerning the matter that Jews and Christians are foul?" "Yes, they are foul," he said. "It is necessary to keep away from them." When I asked the reason why, he replied, "It is done so in retaliation for an insult. For they look on us as disbelievers and deny our Prophet Muhammad 'alaihis-salâm'. We therefore retaliate for this." I said to him, "Dear teacher, isn't cleanliness an issue of îmân? Despite this fact, the avenues and streets around the **Sahn-i-sherîf** [the area surrounding hadrat 'Alî's mausoleum] are not clean. Even the madrasas, which are the places of knowledge, cannot be said to be clean." He replied, "Yes, it is true; cleanliness is from îmân. Yet it cannot be helped because the Shiites are negligent about cleanliness."

The answers given by this man in the Ministry were precisely concurrent with the answers I had received

---

[28] Teaching, preaching, and commending the Islamic commandments.

[29] Admonishing, warning against the Islamic prohibitions.

from the Shiite scholar in Najaf. Such accurate identity between this man and the scholar in Najaf amazed me utterly. In addition, this man spoke Persian.

The secretary said, "If you had met the archetypes of the other four personages, you would talk to their imitations now and see how identical they are with their originals." When I said, "I know how the Shaikh-ul-islâm thinks. For Ahmed Efendi, my hodja in Istanbul, gave a detailed description of the Shaikh-ul-islâm to me," the secretary said, "Then you can go ahead and talk with his model."

I went near the Shaikh-ul-islâm's model and said to him, "Is it fard to obey the Khalîfa?" "Yes, it is wâjib," he replied. "It is wâjib, as it is fard to obey Allah and the Prophet." When I asked what evidence he had to prove this, he answered, "Didn't you hear about Janâb-i-Allah's âyat, **'Obey Allah, His Prophet, and the Ulul amr from among you'?**"[30] I said, "Does this mean that Allah commands us to obey the Khalîfa Yazîd, who permitted his army to plunder Medîna and who killed our Prophet's grandson Huseyn, and Walîd who drank alcoholic spirits?" His answer was this: "My son! Yazîd was the Amîr-ul-mu'minîn with Allah's permission. He did not command the killing of Huseyn. Do not believe in the Shiite lies! Read the books well! He made a mistake. Then he made tawba for this (he repented and begged for Allah's forgiveness and mercy). He was right about his ordering Medina-i-munawwara plundered. For the inhabitants of Medina had become quite unbridled and disobedient. As for

---

[30] Nisâ sûra, âyat: 59

Walîd; yes, he was a sinner. It is not wâjib to imitate the Khalîfa, but to obey his commandments compatible with the Sharî'at." I had asked these same questions to my hodja Ahmed Efendi and received identical answers with slight differences.

Then I asked the secretary, "What are the ultimate reasons for preparing these models?" He said, "With this method we are assessing the mental capacities of the (Ottoman) Sultan and the Muslim scholars, be they Shi'î or Sunnî. We are searching for the measures that will help us cope with them. For instance, if you know what direction the enemy forces will come from, you will make preparations accordingly, post your forces at suitable positions, and thus rout the enemy. On the other hand, if you aren't sure about the direction of the enemy assault you will spread your forces here and there in a haphazard way and suffer a defeat. ... By the same token, if you know the evidences Muslims will furnish to prove that their faith, their madh-hab is right, it will be possible for you to prepare the counter-evidences to rebut their evidences and undermine their belief with those counter-evidences."

Then he gave me a book of one thousand pages containing the results of the observations and projects carried out by the aforenamed five representative men in areas such as military, finance, education, and religion. He said, "Please read this book and return it to us." I took the book home with me. I read through it with utmost attention during my three-week holiday.

The book was of a wonderful sort. For the important answers and the delicate observations it contained sounded genuine. I think that the answers given by the representative five men were more than seventy percent agreeable with the answers that their archetypes would have given. Indeed, the secretary had said that the answers were seventy percent correct.

Having read the book, I now had more confidence in my State and I knew for certain that the plans for demolishing the Ottoman Empire in time shorter than a century had already been prepared. The secretary also said, "In other similar rooms we have identical tables intended for countries we have been colonizing as well as for those we are planning to colonize."

When I asked the secretary where they found such diligent and talented men, he replied, "Our agents all over the world are providing us intelligence continuously. As you see, these representatives are experts in their work. Naturally, if you were furnished with all the information possessed by a particular person, you would be able to think like him and to make the decisions he would make. For you would be his substitute now."

The secretary went on, "So this was the first secret I was ordered by the Ministry to give you.

"I shall tell you the second secret a month later, when you return the book of one thousand pages."

I read the book part by part from the beginning to the end, focusing all my attention on it. It increased my information about the Muhammadans. Now I knew how they thought, what their weaknesses were, what made them powerful, and how to transform their powerful qualities into vulnerable spots.

Muslims' weak spots as recorded in the book were as follows:

1- The Sunnite-Shiite controversy; the sovereign-people controversy;[31] the Turkish-Iranian controversy; the tribal controversy; and the scholars-states controversy.[32]

2- With very few exceptions, Muslims are ignorant and illiterate.[33]

3- Lack of spirituality, knowledge, and conscience.[34] They have completely ceased from worldly

---

[31] This assertion is entirely wrong. It contradicts his former statement that "it is fard to obey the Pâdishâh."

[32] This is sheer calumniation. The written will of Osmân ('Uthmân) Ghâzî, (the first Ottoman Pâdishâh), is a detailed example of the value and honour the Ottoman administration set on the scholars. All the Pâdishâhs granted the highest positions to the scholars. When the jealous adversaries of Mawlânâ Khâlid Baghdâdî slanderously denounced him to Mahmûd Khân II and demanded that he be executed, the Sultan gave this widely known answer: "Scholars would by no means be harmful to the State." The Ottoman Sultans granted a house, provisions, and a high salary to every scholar.

[33] The books on religion, ethics, îmân, and science written by thousands of Ottoman scholars are known universally. Peasants, who are supposed to be the most illiterate sort of people, were very well informed of their faith, worships, and craft. There were mosques, schools, and madrasas in all villages. Villagers were taught how to read and write, religious and worldly knowledge in these places. Women in villages knew how to read Qur'ân al-kerîm. Most scholars and Awliyâ were brought up and educated in villages.

[34] The Ottoman Muslims were very firm spiritually. The people would run for Jihâd in order to attain martyrdom. After each of the (five) daily

business and are absorbed in matters pertaining to the Hereafter.[35]

4-   The emperors are cruel dictators.[36]

5-   The roads are unsafe, transportation and travels are sporadic.[37]

6-   No precaution is taken against epidemics such as plague and cholera, which kill tens of thousands of people each year; hygiene is altogether ignored.[38]

7-   The cities are in ruins, and there is no system of

---

prayers of namâz, as well as during every Friday Khutba, the religious men would pronounce benedictions over the Khalîfa and the State, and the whole congregation would say "Âmîn". Christian villagers, on the other hand, are mostly illiterate, totally unaware of their faith and worldly knowledge, and therefore take the priests' sermons for granted and adhere to the lies and superstitions they have fabricated in the name of religion. They are like senseless flocks of animals.

[35] Unlike Christianity, Islam does not separate the religion from the world. It is an act of worship to busy oneself with worldly matters. Our Prophet stated, "Work for the world as though you would never die, and (work) for the Hereafter as if you were going to die tomorrow."

[36] The emperors brought pressure to bear on the people for the execution of the principles of the Sharî'at. They did not perpetrate oppression like the European kings.

[37] The roads were so safe that a Muslim who set out from Bosnia would travel as far as Mekka comfortably and free of charge, staying, eating and drinking in the villages on the way, and the villagers would most of the time give him presents.

[38] There were hospitals and asylums everywhere. Even Napoleon was cured by the Ottomans. All Muslims adapt themselves to the hadîth-i-sherîf, "He who has îmân will be clean."

supplying water.[39]

8- The administration is unable to cope with rebels and insurgents, there is a general disorderliness, rules of the Qur'ân, of which they are so proud, are almost never put into practice.[40]

9- Economical   collapse,   poverty,   and retrogression.

10- There is not an orderly army, nor adequate weaponry; and the weapons in stock are classical and friable. [Are they unaware of the systematic army established by Orhan Ghâzî, who ascended to the (Ottoman) throne in 726 (C.E. 1326), Yıldırım (The Thunderbolt) Bâyezîd Khan's immaculate army, which routed the great army of crusaders in Nighbolu in 799 (C.E. 1399)?]

11- Violation of women's right.[41]

12- Lack of environmental health and cleanliness.[42]

---

[39] These slanders are not even worth answering. Fîrûz Shâh, the Sultan of Delhi, passed away in 790 [C.E. 1388]. The orchards and gardens irrigated by the wide 240 km canal constructed with his command relapsed into a wasteland during the British invasion. The remains of the Ottoman architecture are still dazzling the eyes of tourists.

[40] They must be confusing the Ottomans with those French generals who were awarded for pouring their kings' excrement into Seine.

[41] At a time when the British were totally oblivious to arts, weaponry, and women's rights, the Ottomans formulated these concepts in the most exquisite way. Would they have the face to deny the fact that the Swedish and the French kings asked for help from the Ottomans?

After citing what was considered as Muslims' vulnerable spots in the paragraphs paraphrased above, the book advised to cause Muslims to remain oblivious of the material and spiritual superiority of their faith, Islam. Then, it gave the following information about Islam:

1- Islam commands unity and cooperation and prohibits disunion. It is stated in the Qur'ân, **"Hold fast to Allah's rope altogether."**[43]

2- Islam commands being educated and being conscious. It is stated in the Qur'ân, **"Travel on the earth."**[44]

3- Islam commands acquiring knowledge. It is stated in a hadîth, **"Learning knowledge is fard for every Muslim, male and female alike."**

4- Islam commands working for the world. It is stated in the Qur'ân, **"Some of them: O our Allah! Allot to us whatever is beautiful both in the world and in the Hereafter."**[45]

5- Islam commands consultation. It is stated in the Qur'ân, **"Their deeds are** (done) **upon consultation**

---

[42] The streets were extremely clean. In fact, there were health services allotted to cleaning the spittles in the streets.

[43] Âl-i-'Imrân sûra, âyat: 103.

[44] Âl-i-'Imrân sûra, âyat: 137.

[45] Baqara sûra, âyat: 201.

among themselves."[46]

6- Islam commands to build roads. It is stated in the Qur'ân, **"Walk on the earth."**[47]

7- Islam commands Muslims to maintain their health. It is stated in a hadîth, **"Knowledge is** (made up) **of four** (parts): **1) The knowledge of Fiqh for the maintenance of faith; 2) The knowledge of Medicine for the maintenance of health; 3) The knowledge of Sarf and Nahw** (Arabic grammar) **for the maintenance of language; 4) The knowledge of Astronomy so as to be aware of the times."**

8- Islam commands development. It is stated in the Qur'ân, **"Allah created everything on the earth for you."**[48]

9- Islam commands orderliness. It is stated in the Qur'ân, **"Everything is based on calculations, orders."**[49]

10- Islam commands being strong economically. It is stated in a hadîth. **"Work for your world as though you would never die. And work for your hereafter as if you were going to die tomorrow."**

---

[46] Shûrâ sûra, âyat: 38.

[47] Mulk: 15.

[48] Baqâra sûra, âyat: 29.

[49] Hijr: 19.

11- Islam commands establishing an army equipped with powerful weapons. It is stated in the Qur'ân, **"Prepare as many forces as you can against them."**[50]

12- Islam commands observing women's rights and to value them. It is stated in the Qur'ân, **"As men legally have** (rights) **over women, so women have rights over them."**[51]

13- Islam commands cleanliness. It is stated in a hadîth, **"Cleanliness is from îmân."**

The book recommended degenerating and impairing the following power sources:

1- Islam has negated racial, lingual, traditional, conventional, and national bigotry.

2- Interest, profiteering, fornication, alcoholic spirits, and pork are forbidden.

3- Muslims are firmly adherent to their 'Ulamâ (religious scholars).

4- Most of the Sunnî Muslims accept the Khalîfa as the Prophet's representative. They believe that it is fard to show him the same respect as must be shown to Allah and the Prophet.

---

[50] Enfâl sûra, âyat: 60.

[51] Baqara sûra, âyat: 228.

5-   Jihâd is fard.

6-   According to the Shî'î Muslims, all non-Muslims and Sunnî Muslims are foul people.

7-   All Muslims believe that Islam is the only true religion.

8-   Most Muslims believe that it is fard to expel the Jews and Christians from the Arab peninsula.

9-   They perform their worships, (such as namâz, fast, hajj...), in the most beautiful way.

10-   The Shî'î Muslims believe that it is harâm (forbidden) to build churches in Muslim countries.

11-   Muslims hold fast to the principles of the Islamic belief.

12-   The Shî'î Muslims consider it fard to give one-fifth of the **Humus,** i.e. booties taken in Holy War, to the 'Ulamâ.

13-   Muslims raise their children with such education that they are not likely to abandon the way followed by their ancestors.

14-   Muslim women cover themselves so well that mischief can by no means act on them.

15-   Muslims make namâz in jamâ'at, which brings them together five times daily.

16- Because the Prophet's grave and those of 'Alî and other pious Muslims are sacred according to them, they assemble at these places.

17- There are a number of people descending from the Prophet, [who are called Sayyids and Sherîfs]; these people remind of the Prophet and keep Him always remain alive in the eyes of Muslims.

18- When Muslims assemble, preachers consolidate their îmân and motivate them to do pious acts.

19- It is fard to perform Amr-i-bi-l-ma'rûf [advising piety] and nahy-i-ani-l-munkar [admonishing against wrongdoing].

20- It is sunnat to marry more than one women in order to contribute to the increase of Muslim population.

21- Converting one person to Islam is more valuable to a Muslim than possessing the whole world.

22- The hadîth, **"If a person opens an auspicious way, he will attain the thawâbs of people who follow that way as well as the thawâb for having attained it,"** is well known among Muslims.

23- Muslims hold the Qur'ân and hadîths in very profound reverence. They believe that obeying these sources is the only way of attaining Paradise.

The book recommended to vitiate Muslims' staunch spots and to popularize their weaknesses, and it prescribed the methods for accomplishing this.

It advised the following steps for popularizing their vulnerable spots:

1- Establish controversies by inducing animosity among disputing groups, inoculating mistrust, and by publishing literature to further incite controversies.

2- Obstruct schooling and publications, and burn literature whenever possible. Make sure that Muslim children remain ignorant by casting various aspersions on religious authorities and thus preventing Muslim parents from sending their children to religious schools. [This British method has been very harmful to Islam.]

3-4- Praise Paradise in their presence and convince them that they need not work for a worldly life. Enlarge the circles of Tasawwuf. Keep them in an unconscious state by encouraging them to read books advising **Zuhd,** such as **Ihyâ-ul-'ulûm-id-dîn,** by Ghazâlî, **Mesnevî,** by Mawlânâ, and various books written by Muhyiddîn Arabî.[52]

5- Wheedle the emperors into cruelty and dictatorship by the following demagogic falsifications: You are Allah's shadows on the earth. In fact, Abû Bakr, 'Umar, 'Uthmân, 'Alî, Umayyads and Abbasids came to seize power by sheer force and the sword, and

---

[52] Zuhd, which is commended by books of Tasawwuf, does not mean to cease from worldly labour. It means not to be fond of the world. In other words, working for the world, earning worldly needs, and using them compatibly with the Sharî'at will provide as much thawâb as other acts of worship will.

each of them was a sovereign. For example, Abû Bakr assumed power with the help of 'Umar's sword and by setting fire to the houses of those who would not obey him, such as Fâtima's house.[53]

And 'Umar became Khalîfa upon Abû Bakr's commendation. 'Uthmân, on the other hand, became the president with 'Umar's order. As for 'Alî; he became head of the State by an election held among bandits. Muâwiya assumed power by the sword.[54] Then, in the time of the Umayyads, sovereignty was turned into an

---

[53] There are indications in hadîth-i-sherîfs that Abû Bakr, 'Umar, 'Uthmân, and 'Alî 'radiy-Allâhu anhum' would become Khalîfas. Yet there is not a clear statement concerning their times. Rasûlullah 'sall- Allâhu alaihi wa sallam' left this matter to his Sahâba's choice. The Sahâba had three different kinds of ijtihâd in electing the Khalîfa. Caliphate was not a property to be inherited by one's relatives. Abû Bakr, who had been the first person to become a Muslim, who had caused others to become Believers, behind whom our Prophet had performed namâz by telling him to be the imâm and conduct the namâz, and with whom the Prophet had migrated (to Medina), was the most suitable candidate. Some (of the Sahâba) went to hadrat 'Alî's place. One of them, namely, Abû Sufyân, said, "Hold out your hand! I shall pay homage to you! If you like, I shall fill all the place with cavalrymen and infantrymen." Hadrat 'Alî refused this, answering, "Are you trying to break the Muslims into groups? My staying home is not intended for being elected Khalîfa. Bereavement from Rasûlullah has shocked me. I feel demented." He went to the mosque. He paid homage to Abû Bakr in the presence of all the others. Upon this Abû Bakr said, "I don't want to be Khalîfa. I accept it willy-nilly to prevent confusion." 'Alî replied, "You are more worthy of being Khalîfa." The statements of praise hadrat 'Alî made of Abû Bakr that day are quoted in our (Turkish) book **Se'âdet-i Ebediyye.** Hadrat 'Umar accompanied hadrat 'Alî to his house. Hadrat 'Alî would say, "After Rasûlullah, Abû Bakr and 'Umar are the highest of this Ummat (Muslims)." People who believed the Shiite lies and slanders are responsible for the wretched state Muslims are in today. The British are still pushing on this instigation.

[54] Hadrat Muâwiya became Khalîfa upon hadrat Hasan's paying homage to him. Please read the book Documents of the Right Word.

inheritance transferred through paternal chain. So was the case with the Abbasids. These are the evidences for the fact that in Islam sovereignty is a form of dictatorship.

6- Delete death penalty for homicide from the penal code. [Death punishment is the only deterrent to homicide and banditry. Anarchy and banditry cannot be prevented without death penalty.] Hinder the administration in punishing highwaymen and robbers. Make sure that travelling is unsafe by supporting and arming them.

7- We can make them lead an unhealthy life with the following scheme: Everything is dependent on Allah's foreordination. Medical treatment will have no role in restoring health. Does not Allah say in the Qur'ân, **"My Rabb (Allah) makes me eat and drink. He cures me when I am ill. He alone will kill me and then resurrect me."**[55] Then, no one will recover from an illness or escape death outside Allah's will.[56]

---

[55] Shûrâ sûra, âyats: 79-80-81

[56] British agents distort the meanings of âyat-i-kerîmas and hadîth-i-sherîfs in order to mislead Muslims. It is sunnat (something done, advised, recommended, liked by the Prophet) to have medical treatment. Allâhu ta'âlâ has created a curing effect in medicine. Our Prophet commanded to take medicine. Allâhu ta'âlâ, the creator of everything, is the healer. Yet He has created a law of causation and commands us to obey this law by holding on to the causes. We must work hard, discover the causes, and use them. To say, "He cures me," means to say, "He gives me the means that will cause healing." It is a commandment (of Islam) to do research to discover the causes. Our Prophet stated, "It is farz both for men and for women to study and acquire knowledge." At another time he stated, "Allâhu ta'âlâ likes those who work and earn."

HEMPHER

8-   Make the following statements for encouraging cruelty: Islam is a religion of worship. It has no interest in State matters. Therefore, Muhammad and his Khalîfas did not have any ministers or laws.[57]

9-   Economic decline is a natural consequence of the injurious activities advised so far. We can add to the atrophy by rotting the crops, sinking the trade ships, setting fire to the market places, destroying dams and barrages and thus leaving agricultural areas and industrial centers under water, and finally by contaminating their networks of drinking water.[58]

10- Accustom statesmen to such indulgences as [sex, sports,] alcohol, gambling, corruption which cause sedition and intriguing, and spending the State property for their personal advantages. Encourage the civil servants to do things of this sort and reward those who serve us in this way.

Then the book added the following advice: The British spies assigned this duty must be protected secretly or openly, and no expense must be spared to rescue the ones arrested by Muslims.

11- Popularize all sorts of interest. For interest not only ruins national economy, but also accustoms Muslims to disobeying the Koranic rules. Once a

---

[57] Worship does not only consist of namâz, fast and hajj. It is also worship to do worldly business because Allâhu ta'âlâ commands it but in a manner compatible with the Sharî'at. It is very thawâb (deserving reward in the Hereafter) to work for useful things.

[58] See the savagery, the cruelty perpetrated by the British, who call themselves civilized and repeat the phrase 'human rights' so often!

person has violated one article of law, it will be easy for him to violate the other articles, too. They must be told that "interest is harâm when in multiples, for it is stated in the Qur'ân, **'Do not receive interest in multiples.'**[59] Therefore, not every form of interest is harâm." [The pay-off time of a loan must not be appointed in advance. Any extra payment agreed on (at the time of lending) is interest. This type of interest is a grave sin, be the extra payment stipulated worth only a dirham. If it is stipulated that the same amount (borrowed) must be repaid after a certain time, this is interest according to the Hanafî madh-hab. In sales on credit, time of repayment must be appointed; yet if the debtor cannot pay off at the appointed time and the time is protracted and an extra payment is stipulated, this kind of interest is called **Mudâ'af.** The âyat-i-karîma quoted above states this type of interest in trade.]

12- Spread false charges of atrocity against scholars, cast sordid aspersions against them and thus alienate Muslims from them. We shall disguise some of our spies as them. Then we shall have them commit squalid deeds. Thus they will be confused with scholars and every scholar will be looked upon with suspicion. It is a must to infiltrate these spies into Al-Az-har, Istanbul, Najaf, and Kerbelâ. We shall open schools, colleges for estranging Muslims from scholars. In these schools we shall educate Byzantine, Greek and Armenian children and bring them up as the enemies of Muslims. As for Muslim children; we shall imbue them with the conviction that their ancestors were ignorant people. In order to make these children hostile towards Khalîfas,

---

[59] Âl-i-'Imrân sûra, âyat: 130.

scholars, and statesmen, we shall tell them about their errors and convince them that they were busy with their sensuous pleasures, that Khalîfas spent their time having fun with concubines, that they misused the people's property, that they did not obey the Prophet in anything they did.

In order to spread the calumniation that Islam abhors womankind, we shall quote the âyat, **"Men are dominant over women,"**[60] and the hadîth, **"The woman is an evil altogether."**[61]

---

[60] Nisâ sûra, âyat: 34

[61] It is stated in a hadîth-i-sharîf, **"A woman** (wife) **who obeys the Sharî'at is one of the blessings of Paradise. A woman who follows her sensations and disobeys the Sharî'at is evil."** A poor single woman's father has to subsist her, be her unmarried or widowed. If he does not, he is to be imprisoned. If she does not have a father, or if her father is (too) poor (to subsist her), her mahram relatives will (have to) care for her. In case she does not have such relatives, either, the government will have to allot a salary for her. A Muslim woman will never have to work for a living. The Islamic religion has burdened man with all the needs of his woman. In return for this heavy burden, man might as well have been made the only inheritor of his progenitors; yet, as another kindness toward womankind, Allâhu ta'âlâ has commanded that they should be given half the property inherited by their brothers. A husband cannot force his wife to work within or without the house. If a woman wants to work, she can do so with her husband's permission, with the proviso that she should be covered and there should not be men at the place where she works; and in this case her earnings will belong to her. No one can force a woman to relinquish earnings of this sort or property she has inherited or the mehr (she has deserved through marriage agreement). Nor can she be forced to spend it for her or her children's needs or for anything needed in the house. It is fard for the husband to provide all such needs. In today's communist regimes, women as well as men are made to work in the heaviest jobs for food only, like animals. In Christian countries, said to be free world countries, and in some Arabic countries said to be Muslim countries, women work like men in factories, in fields, in trade businesses under the sophistry that "life is common." As it frequently appears in daily newspapers, most of them regret having

13- Dirtiness is the result of lack of water. Therefore, we must deter the increasing of the water supplies under various schemes.

The book advised the following steps for destroying Muslims' strongholds:

1- Induce such chauvinistic devotions as racism and nationalism among Muslims so as to retract their attention towards their pre- Islamic heroisms. Rejuvenate the Pharaoh period in Egypt, the Magi period in Iran, the Babylonian period in Iraq, the Attila and Dzengiz era [tyrannisms] in the Ottomans. [They contained a long list on this subject.]

---

married, so that law courts teem with files of divorce suits. Utterances spoken by the blessed mouth of the Messenger of Allah are of three kinds: The first kind comprises utterances which come from Allâhu ta'âlâ both in tenor and in vehicle. These utterances are called **âyat-i-kerîma**, which make up the **Qur'ân al-kerîm** collectively. The utterance, **"Every good and useful thing coming to you is willed and sent by Allâhu ta'âlâ. Every evil and harmful thing is wished by your nafs. All these things are created and sent by Allâhu ta'âlâ,"** is the seventy-eighth âyat of **Nisâ** sûra. The second kind includes utterances whose words belong to our Prophet while their meanings are inspired by Allâhu ta'âlâ. These utterances are called **hadîth-i-qudsî.** The utterance, **"Be inimical towards your nafs. For it is My enemy,"** is a hadîth-i-qudsî. In the third kind are those utterances belonging to our Prophet both in wording and in meaning. They are called **hadîth-i sherîf.** The utterance, **"A woman who obeys the Sharî'at is one of the blessings of Paradise. A woman who follows her nafs is evil,"** is a hadîth-i-sherîf. Hadrat Muhyiddîn-i-Arabî explains this hadîth-i-sherîf in the first volume of his book **Musâmarât.** The British spy withholds the first half of the hadîth and reveals only the latter half. If women all over the world knew about the value, the comfort and peace, the freedom and the right to divorce Islam has conferred on them, they would immediately become Muslims and endeavour to disseminate Islam all over the world. It is a shame that they cannot realise these facts. May Allâhu ta'âlâ bless all humanity with the fortune of learning Islam's luminous way correctly!

2- The following vices must be done secretly or publicly: Alcoholic spirits, gambling, fornication, pork, [and fights among sports clubs.] In doing this, Christians, Jews, Magians, and other non-Muslims living in Muslim countries should be utilized to a maximum, and those who work for this purpose should be awarded high salaries by the treasury tepartment of the Ministry of the Commonwealth.

3- Sow suspicion among them concerning Jihâd; convince them that Jihâd was a temporary commandment and that it has been outdated.

4- Dispel the notion that "disbelievers are foul" from the hearts of Shiites. Quote the Koranic verse, **"As the food of those given a** (heavenly) **Book is halâl for you, so is your food halâl for them,"**[62] and tell them that the Prophet had a Jewish wife named Sâfiyya and a Christian wife named Mâriya and that the Prophet's wives were not foul at all.[63]

5- Imbue Muslims with the belief that "what the Prophet meant by 'Islam' was 'a perfect religion' and therefore this religion could be Judaism or Christianity

---

[62] Mâida sûra, âyat: 5.

[63] Hadrat Sâfiyya, whom the British call a Jew, had already become a Muslim (when she married our Prophet). As for Mâriya, an Egyptian, she was not one of the blessed wives of the Messenger of Allah. She was a jâriya. She, too, was a Muslim. (When she passed away), 'Umar 'radiy-Allâhu anh', who was the Khalîfa at that time, conducted the ritual prayer (performed when a Muslim dies). According to the belief of Ahl as-sunna, a Christian woman can be a jâriya as well as a wife (for a Muslim man). Contrary to the Shiite credo (in this respect), disbelievers are not foul themselves. What is foul in them is the belief they hold.

as well as Islam." Substantiate this with the following reasoning: The Qur'ân gives the name 'Muslim' to members of all religions. For instance, it quotes the Prophet Joseph(Yûsuf 'alaihis-salâm') as having invoked, **"Kill me as a Muslim,"**[64] and the Prophets Ibrâhîm and Ismâ'îl as having prayed, "O our Rabb (Allah)! Make us Muslims for Yourself and make a Muslim people for Yourself from among our offspring,"[65] and the Prophet Ya'qûb as having said to his sons, "Die only and only as Muslims."[66]

6-   Repeat frequently that it is not harâm to build churches, that the Prophet and his Khalîfas did not

---

[64] Belief in the information a Prophet has brought from Allâhu ta'âlâ is called Îmân. The information to be believed is of two sorts: (1) Information to be believed only; (2) Information both to be believed and to be practised. The first sort of information, which is the basis of îmân, comprises six tenets. All Prophets taught the same basic principles of îmân. Today, all the Jews, Christians, scientists, statesmen, commanders all over the world, and all these so-called modernists believe in the Hereafter, that is, in resurrection after death. Those who call themselves modern people have to believe, like these people. On the other hand, Prophets' Sharî'ats, i.e. the commandments and prohibitions in their religions, are not the same. Having îmân and adapting oneself to the Sharî'at is called **Islam.** Since each Prophet has a different Sharî'at, the Islam of each Prophet is different from that of another. Each Messenger of Allah brought a new Islam, abrogating the Islam of the Prophet prior to him. The Islam brought by the last Prophet Muhammad 'alaihis-salâm' shall remain valid till the end of the world. In the 19th and 85th âyats of surat **Âl-i-'Imrân,** Allâhu ta'âlâ commands Jews and Christians to give up their former Islams. He declares that those who do not adapt themselves to Muhammad 'alaihis-salâm' shall not enter Paradise and that they shall suffer eternal burning in Hell. Each of the aforenamed Prophets, i.e. Ibrâhîm, Ismâ'îl, and Yûsuf, supplicated for the Islam that was valid in his time. Those Islams, going to church, for instance, are not valid today.

[65] Baqara sûra, âyat: 128

[66] Baqara sûra, âyat: 132

demolish them, that on the contrary they respected them, that the Qur'ân states, "If Allah had not dispelled some people by means of others, monasteries, churches, synagogues, and mosques wherein Allah's name is mentioned very much would have been annihilated (by now),"[67] that Islam respects temples, that it does not demolish them, and that it prevents those who would otherwise demolish them.

7- Confuse Muslims about the hadîths, "Deport the Jews from the Arabic Peninsula," and, "Two religions cannot coexist on the Arabic peninsula." Say that "If these two hadîths were true, the Prophet would not have had a Jewish wife and a Christian one. Nor would he have made an agreement with the Najran Christians."[68]

8- Try to hamper Muslims in their worships and make them falter about the usefulness of worships by saying that "Allah does not need men's worships."[69] Prevent them from their worship of hajj as well as from any sort of worship that will bring them together. Likewise, try to obstruct construction of mosques, mausoleums and madrasas and the restoration of Ka'ba.

9- Mystify the Shiites about the rule that one-fifth

---

[67] Hajj sûra, âyat: 40

[68] See the footnote 2 on page 56.

[69] Worships are performed because Allâhu ta'âlâ has commanded them. Yes, Allâhu ta'âlâ does not need His born slaves' worships. Yet the born slaves themselves need worshipping. These people (Christians) go to church in crowds. On the other hand they prevent Muslims from going to mosques.

of the ghanîma property taken from the enemy in combat is to be given to the 'Ulamâ and explain that this one-fifth belongs to the ghanîma property taken from (Dâr-ul-harb) and that it has nothing to do with commercial earnings. Then add that "Humus (the one-fifth mentioned above) is to be given to the Prophet or to the Khalîfa, not to the 'Ulamâ. For the 'Ulamâ are given houses, palaces, animals, and orchards. Therefore, it is not permissible to give them the (Humus)."

10- Insert heresies into Muslims' credal tenets and then criticize Islam for being a religion of terror. Assert that Muslim countries are retrogressive and that they have undergone shocks, thus impairing their adherence to Islam. [On the other hand, Muslims established the greatest and the most civilized empire of the world. They declined as their adherence to Islam deteriorated.]

11- Very important! Alienate children from their fathers, thus depriving them of their elders' education. We shall educate them. Consequently, the moment children have parted from their fathers' education, there will no longer be any possibility for them to maintain contact with their belief, faith, or religious scholars.

12- Provoke the womenfolk to get rid of their traditional covers. Fabricate such falsifications as "Covering is not a genuine Islamic commandment. It is a tradition established in the time of the Abbasids. Formerly, other people would see the Prophet's wives and women would join all sorts of social activities." After stripping the woman of her traditional cover, tempt the youth towards her and cause indecencies between them! This is a very effective method for annihilating Islam. First use non-Muslim women for this purpose. In the course of time the Muslim woman will automatically degenerate and will begin to follow their example.[70]

---

[70] Before the revelation of the âyat of Hijâb (veiling), women would not cover themselves; they would come to the Messenger of Allah, ask him questions, and learn from him what they did not know. Whenever the Messenger of Allah visited one of them in her home, other women would go there, too, sitting, listening, and learning. Six years after the Hijrat Nûr sûra was revealed to prohibit women from sitting or talking with men (other than spouse or other close relatives). From then on, the Messenger of Allah commanded women to learn what they did not know by asking his blessed wives. These disbelievers are misleading Muslims by withholding the fact that women covered themselves after the revelation of the âyat of Hijâb.

Umm-i Salama 'radiy-Allâhu anha', blessed wife of Rasulullah, narrates: Maymûna 'radiy-Allâhu anha', another wife of Rasulullah 'sall-Allâhu alaihi wa sallam' and I were with the Messenger of Allah 'sall-Allâhu alaihi wa sallam', when Ibn-i-Umm-i-Maktûm 'radiy- Allâhu anh' asked for permission and entered. When the Messenger of Allah 'sall-Allâhu alaihi wa sallam' saw him he said to us, **"Withdraw behind the curtain!"** When I said, "Isn't he blind? He won't see us," the Messenger of Allah answered, **"Are you blind, too? Don't you see him?"** That is, he meant, "He may be blind, but you aren't." This hadîth-i-sherîf was quoted by Imâm-i-Ahmad and Tirmuzî and Abû Dâwûd 'rahimahumullâhi ta'âlâ.' According to this hadîth-i-sherîf, as it is harâm for a man to look at a woman who is not his spouse or a close relative, so is it harâm for a woman to look at a man who is not her spouse or a close relative. Our madh-hab imâms took other hadîth-i-sherîfs into consideration as well, and said that "It is harâm for a woman to look at a nâ-mahram man's **awrat** parts. It is easy to do this. These easy commandments and prohibitions are called (Rukhsat). It is **Azimat** for a woman not to look at a nâ- mahram man's head and hair. A man's awrat part for a woman (the part which is forbidden for a woman to look at) is between his knee and navel. And (obeying) this (rule only, without paying attention to the Azîmat), is (called) **Rukhsât.** As is seen, the Azwâj-i-tâhirat (the pure wives of the Messenger of Allah) 'radiy-Allâhu ta'âlâ anhunna' and the As-hâb-i-kirâm 'radiy-Allâhu anhum' would always act on the Azîmat and they would refrain from the Rukhsât. The **Zindiqs** who try to destroy Islam from within put forward the fact that women did not cover themselves before the revelation of the âyat of Hijâb and say that "Women did not cover themselves in the Prophet's time. Women's veiling themselves like ogres, a practice which is so common

13- Exploit every opportunity to put an end to performing namâz in jamâ'at by casting aspersions on

today, did not exist at that time. Hadrat Âisha, for one, would go out bare headed. Today's practice of veiling was invented by the bigoted men of fiqh afterwards." The hadîth-i-sherîfs quoted above show clearly that these statements of theirs are lies and slanders.

The four right Madh-habs, which are the explanations of the commandments and prohibitions of Allâhu ta'âlâ, give different accounts pertaining to men's **awrat** parts, that is, parts of their body which are forbidden (for others) to look at or (for them) to show to others. It is fard for every man to cover those parts of his body which the Madh-hab he is in prescribes to be harâm. It is harâm to look at someone else's parts of awrat. The following hadîth-i-sherîfs are written in the book **Eshi'at-ul-leme'at:**

"Let men and women not look at the awrat parts of people of their own sex." In the Hanafî Madh-hab, a man's parts of awrat for other men are the same as those of a woman for other women: the area between the knees and the navel. A woman's parts of awrat for men nâ-mahram to her, on the other hand, are all her body with the exception of the hands and face. (Any member of the opposite sex who is not one of a person's close relatives called mahram is called nâ-mahram. Islam names one's mahram relatives. They are eighteen). A woman's hair is within her parts of awrat. It is harâm to look at someone's parts of awrat even without any feeling of lust.

"If you see a woman, turn your face away from her! Although it is not sinful to see one unexpectedly, it is sinful to look at her again."
"O 'Alî! Do not open your thigh! Do not look at someone else's thigh, be it a corpse or a person who is alive."
"May Allah curse those who open their parts and those who look at them!"
"A person who makes himself like a community will become one of them." This hadîth-i-sherîf shows that a person who adapts himself to enemies of Islam in ethics, behaviour or styles of dressing will become one of them. Those who adapt themselves to disbelievers' wicked fashions, who name harâms 'fine arts', and who call people who commit harâms 'artists', should take this hadîth-i-sherîf as a warning. It is written as follows in **Kimyâ-i-sa'âdat:** "It is harâm for women and girls to go out without covering their heads, hair, arms and legs or in thin, ornamented, tight, perfumed dresses. If a woman's parents, husband or brothers condone her going out in this manner, they will share her sin and the torment (she will suffer for this sin in the Hereafter)." If they make tawba they will be pardoned. Allâhu ta'âlâ likes those who make tawba.

the imâms in mosques, by revealing their mistakes, and by sowing discord and adversity between them and the jamâ'ats (groups of Muslims) who perform their daily prayers of namâz behind them.

14- Say that all mausoleums must be demolished to the ground, that they did not exist in the Prophet's time. In addition, deter Muslims from visiting the graves of Prophets, Khalîfas and pious Muslims by arising doubts about visiting graves. For instance, say, "The Prophet was buried beside his mother and Abû Bekr and 'Umar were buried in the cemetery called Bâkî'.'Uthmân's grave is unknown. Huseyn's head was buried at (a place called) Hannana. It is not known where his body was buried. The graves in Kâzimiyya belong to two caliphs. They do not belong to Kâzim and Jawâd, two descendants of the Prophet. As to the one in Tus (city); that grave belongs to Hârun, not to Ridâ, a member of the Ahl-i-Bayt (the Prophet's Family). The graves in Samerra belong to the Abbasids. They do not belong to Hâdî, Askerî, and Mahdî, members of the Ahl-i-Bayt. As it is fard to demolish all the mausoleums and domes in Muslim countries, so is it a must to bulldoze the cemetery called Bâkî'."

15- Make people feel sceptical about the fact that Sayyids are the Prophet's descendants. Mix Sayyids with other people by making non-Sayyids wear black and green turbans. Thus people will be perplexed in this matter and will consequently begin to distrust Sayyids. Strip religious authorities and Sayyids of their turbans so that the Prophetic pedigree will be lost and religious authorities will not be respected any more.[71]

16- Say that it is fard to demolish the places where Shiites mourn, that this practice is a heresy and aberration. People should be prevented from visiting those places, the number of preachers should be decreased and taxes should be levied on preachers and owners of the places for mourning.

17- Under the pretext of love of freedom, convince all Muslims that "Everyone is free to do whatever he

---

[71] Sayyid Abd-ul-Hakîm Arwâsî 'rahmatullâhi alaih', a great scholar, states in the book **(As-hâb-i-kirâm),** which he wrote in Istanbul: "Hadrat Fâtimâ, the blessed daughter of the Messenger of Allah, and all her offspring till the end of the world are members of the Ahl-i- Bayt. It is necessary to love them even if they are disobedient Muslims. Loving them, helping them with one's heart, body, and/or property, respecting them and observing their rights will cause one to die as a Believer. There was a law court allotted for Sayyids in Hamâ, a city in Syria. In the time of the Abbasid Khalîfas in Egypt, the descendants of Hasan 'radiy-Allâhu anh' were named **Sherîf** and it was decided that they were to wear white turbans, and Huseyn's 'radiy-Allâhu anh' sons were named **Sayyid,** who were to wear green turbans. Children born from these two families were registered in the presence of a judge and two witnesses. During the reign of Sultân Abd-ul-majîd Khân 'rahmatullâhi alaih' Rashîd Pasha, the masonic vizier, cancelled these law courts under the directions of his British bosses. People without any known genealogical origin or religious madh-hab began to be called Sayyid. Bogus Iranian sayyids spread far and wide. It is stated in **Fatâwâ-i-hadîthiyya,** 'In the early days of Islam anyone who was a descendant of the Ahl-i-Bayt was called Sherîf, e.g. Sherîf-i- Abbâsî, Sherîf-i-Zaynalî. Fâtimî Rulers were Shiite. They called only the descendants of Hasan and Huseyn Sherîf. Ashraf Sha'bân bin Huseyn, one of the Turcoman Rulers in Egypt, commanded that Sayyids should wear green turbans so that they be distinguished from Sherîfs. These traditions spread widely, though they do not have any value from the Islamic point of view.' There is detailed information in this subject in **Mir'at-i-kâinât** and in the Turkish version of **Mawâhib- i-ledunniyya** and in the third chapter of the seventh section of the commentary called Zarqânî."

likes. It is not fard to perform Amr-i-bi-l-ma'rûf and Nahy-i-anil-munkar or to teach the Islamic principles." [On the contrary, it is fard to learn and teach Islam. It is a Muslim's first duty.] In addition, imbue them with this conviction: "Christians are to remain in their own faith (Christianity) and Jews are to abide by theirs (Judaism). No one will enter another person's heart. Amr-i-ma'rûf and Nahy-i-anil- munkar are the Khalîfa's duties."

18- In order to impede Muslims from increasing in number, births must be limited and polygamy must be prohibited. Marriage must be subjected to restrictions. For instance, it must be said that an Arab cannot marry an Iranian, an Iranian cannot marry an Arab, a Turk cannot marry an Arab.

19- Make sure to stop Islamic propagations and conversions to Islam. Broadcast the conception that Islam is a religion peculiar to the Arabs only. As an evidence for this, put forward the Koranic verse which reads, "This is a Dhikr for thee and thine people."

20- Pious institutions must be restricted and confined to the State monopoly, to the extent that individuals must be unable to establish madrasas or other similar pious institutions.

21- Arouse doubts as to the authenticity of the Qur'ân in Muslims' minds; publish Koranic translations containing excisions, additions, and interpolations, and then say, "The Qur'ân has been defiled. Its copies are incongruous. A verse one of them contains does not exist in another." Excise the verses insulting Jews, Christians and all other non-Muslims and those commanding Jihâd, Amr-i-bi-l-ma'rûf and Nahy-i-anil munkar.[72]

22- Translate the Qur'ân into other languages such as Turkish, Persian, Indian, thus to prevent Arabic from being learned and read outside Arabic countries, and again, prevent the (Ad-hân), (Namâz), and (Duâ) from being done in Arabic outside of Arabic countries.

Likewise, Muslims will be made to feel doubts about hadîths. The translations, criticisms and interpolations planned for the Qur'ân should be applied to hadîths as well.

When I read through the book, which was entitled **How Can We Demolish Islam,** I found it really excellent. It was a peerless guide for the studies I was going to carry on. When I returned the book to the secretary and told him that it afforded me great

---

[72] These British contrivances came to naught. For Allâhu ta'âlâ has been protecting Qur'ân al-kerîm from interpolation. He did not promise also that He would protect the Injîl (the heavenly Book revealed to hadrat Îsâ). It is for this reason that false books in the name of Bible were written. Even these books were changed in the course of time. The first interpolation in them was made by a Jewish convert named Paul. The greatest of the changes that were made in every century was the one constituted by the three hundred and nineteen priests who convened in Nicea in 325 upon the order of Constantine, the first Roman emperor in Istanbul. In 931 [C.E. 1524], Martin Luther, a German priest, established the Protestant sect. Christians who followed the Pope in Rome were called Catholics. The massacres of Saint Bartholomew and Scotland, the catastrophic mass killings after the tribunals called Inquisition are recorded in Christian history as well. In 446 [C.E. 1054], Michael Kirolarius, Patriarch of Istanbul, dissented from the Pope and established the **Orthodox Church.** The Syrian Monophysite sect was founded by Jacobus (Baradaeus), d. 571 C.E.; the Syrian Maronite sect by Maro, d. 405; and the **Jehovah's Witnesses** by Charles Russell in 1872.

pleasure to read it, he said, "You can be sure that you are not alone in this field. We have lots of men doing the same job as you have been carrying on. Our Ministry has assigned over five thousand men to this mission. The Ministry is considering increasing this number to one hundred thousand. When we reach this number we shall have brought all Muslims under our sway and obtained all Muslim countries."

Sometime later the secretary said: "Good news to you! Our Ministry needs one century at the most to realize this program. We may not live to see those happy days, but our children will. What a beautiful saying this is: 'I have eaten what others sowed. So I am sowing for others.' When the British manage this they will have pleased the entire Christendom and will have rescued them from a twelve-century-old nuisance."

The secretary went on as follows: "The crusading expeditions which continued for centuries were of no use. Nor can the Mongols [armies of Dzengiz] be said to have done anything to extirpate Islam. For their work was sudden, unsystematic, and ungrounded. They carried on military expeditions so as to reveal their enmity. Consequently, they became tired in a short time. But now our valuable administrators are trying to demolish Islam by means of a very subtle plan and a long-range patience.

We must use military force, too. Yet this should be the final phase, that is, after we have completely consumed Islam, after we have hammered it from all directions and rendered it into a miserable state from which it will never recover again and fight against us."

The secretary's final words were these: "Our superiors in Istanbul must have been very wise and intelligent. They executed our plan precisely. What did they do? They mixed with the Muhammadans and opened madrasas for their children. They built churches. They were perfectly sucessful in popularizing alcoholic spirits, gambling, indecencies, and breaking them into groups by means of instigation [and football clubs]. They aroused doubts in the minds of young Muslims. They inserted controversies and oppositions into their governments. They spread mischief everywhere. They depraved administrators, directors, and statesmen by filling their houses with Christian women. With activities of this sort they broke their forces, undermined their adherence to their faith, corrupted them morally, and disrupted their unity and communication. Now the time has come to commence a sudden war and extirpate Islam."[73]

---

[73] The British applied the twenty-one-article destruction plan, which they had prepared in order to annihilate Islam, to the two great Islamic Empires, Indian and Ottoman. They established heretical Islamic groups, such as Wahhabi, Qâdiyânî, Teblîgh-i-jamâ'at, and Jamâ'at-i-Islâmiyya, in India. Then the British army easily invaded India and destroyed the entire Islamic State. They imprisoned the Sultan and butchered his two sons. Extremely valuable articles and the choicest treasures that had been preserved throughout centuries were plundered and shipped to London. They stole the precious stones, such as diamonds, emeralds and rubies, ornamenting the walls of the mausoleum called Taj-mahal, which the Indian Sultan Shâh-i-Jihân had built in 1041 [C.E. 1631] over the grave of his wife Erjumend Beghum in Aghra, plastering their places on the walls with mud. Today these plasters shout out the British savagery to the whole world. And the British are still spending this stolen wealth for the annihilation of Islam. As is expressed by an Islamic poet, "If the cruel have oppression, the oppressed have Allah with them," the divine justice rose and they had their deserts in the Second World War. Fearing that the Germans might invade Britain, most of the wealthy British clergymen, households of Statesmen and ministers, and tens of thousands of enemies

of Islam boarded ships and were on their way to America, when the magnetic mines released from the two German warships of Graf von Spee and two similar ships caught and sank their ships. They all drowned in the Atlantic Ocean. After the war, upon a decision taken by the center of United Nations Human Rights in New York, they receded from their colonies all over the world. They lost most of their sources of income which the Ministry of the Commonwealth had been exploiting for centuries. They were confined to the island called Great Britain. Food and consumer goods were rationed. I remember the Chief of Turkish General Staff, General Salih Omurtak, saying at a dinner party in 1948, "In London, an official guest as I was, I always left the meal table without being fully fed. In Italy, on my way back, I fed myself up by eating plenty of spaghetti." This I am quoting because I was seated opposite the general at the dinner table and I heard exactly what he said. His words are still echoing in my ears. Thenâullâh-i-Dahlawî 'rahmatullâhi aleyh' makes the following observation in his explanation of the eighty- second âyat-i-kerîma of Sûra-i-Mâida: "Muhy-is-sunna Huseyn Beghawî stated that not all Christians are polytheistic. For polytheism means to deify something, i.e. to worship it. Polytheists, like Jews, bear bitter enmity towards Muslims. They kill Muslims, devastating their homelands and demolishing their mosques. They burn copies of Qur'ân al-kerîm." Imâm-i-Rabbânî 'rahmatullâhi aleyh' states in the third letter of the third volume (of his Mektûbât), "A person who worships any being other than Allâhu ta'âlâ is called a polytheist. A person who has not adapted himself to a Prophet's Sharî'at is a polytheist." Christians all over the world today deny Muhammad 'alaihis-salâm' and are therefore disbelievers. Most of them are polytheistic because they say that Îsâ 'alaihis-salâm' is a god, or that he is one of the three gods. Some of them, who profess that "Jesus is a born slave and a prophet of God", are Ahl-i-kitâb (People of the Book). All these people maintain an inimical attitude towards Islam and Muslims. Their attacks were administered by the British. We have been informed in 1412 [1992 A.D.] that the Christians recently concocted ten questions and distributed them in Muslim countries. Islamic savants in Bangladesh by preparing answers to these questions disgraced the Christian priests. **Hakîkat Kitâbevi** in Istanbul, distributes these answers throughout the world under the title of **Al- Ekâzîb-ul-cedîde-tül-Hristiyâniyye.**

Chapter VII

Having enjoyed the first secret, I was looking forward to knowing the second secret. Eventually one day the secretary explained the second secret he had promised. The second secret was a fifty page scheme prepared for the high ranking officials working in the Ministry for annihilating Islam altogether within a century's time. The scheme was comprised of fourteen articles. The scheme was closely guarded for fear that it might be obtained by Muslims. The following are the articles of the scheme:

1- We have to form a well-established alliance and an agreement of mutual help with the Russian Tsar in order to invade Bukhâra, Tâjikistân, Armenia, Khorasan and its neighborhood. Again, a sound agreement must be established with Russians in order to invade their neighbour, Turkey.

2- We must establish cooperation with France in demolishing the Islamic world both from within and from without.

3- We must sow very ardent rows and controversies between the Turkish and Iranian governments and emphasize nationalistic and racist feelings in both parties. In addition, all the Muslim tribes, nations and countries neighbouring one another must be set against one another. All the religious sects, including the extinct ones, must be recovered and set against one another.

4- Parts from Muslim countries must be handed over to non- Muslim communities. For example, Medina must be given to the Jews, Alexandria to the Christians, Imâra to the Sâiba,[74] Kermanshah to the Nusayriya group, who have divinized 'Alî, Mousul to the Yazîdîs, the Iranian gulf to Hindus, Tripoli to the Druzis, Kars to the Alawîs, and Masqat to the Khârijî group. The next step should be to arm these groups so that each of them will be a thorn on the body of Islam. Their areas must be widened till Islam has collapsed and perished.

5- A schedule must be concocted to divide the Muslim and Ottoman States into as small as possible local states that are always at loggerheads with one another. An example of this is today's India. For the following theory is common: "Break, and you will dominate," and "Break, and you will destroy."

6- It is necessary to adulterate Islam's essence by adding interpolated religions and sects into it, and this we must devise in such a subtle manner that the religions we are to invent should be compatible with the sensuous tastes and aspirations of the people among whom we are going to spread them. We shall invent four different religions in the Shiite countries: 1- A religion that divinizes hadrat Huseyn; 2- A religion that divinizes Ja'fer Sâdiq; 3- A religion divinizing Mahdi; 4- A religion divinizing Alî Ridâ. The first one is suitable for Kerbelâ, the second one for Isfahân, the third one for Samarra, and the fourth one for Khorâsân. In the meantime, we must degenerate the existing four Sunnite

---

[74] Sabiens.

madh-habs into four self-standing religions. After doing this, we shall establish an altogether new Islamic sect in Najd, and then instigate bloody rows among all these groups. We shall annihilate the books belonging to the four madh-habs, so that each of these groups will consider themselves to be the only Muslim group and will look on the other groups as heretics that are to be killed.

7- Seeds of mischief and malice, such as fornication, pederasty, alcoholic spirits and gambling, will be scattered among Muslims. Non-Muslims living in the countries concerned will be used for this purpose. A tremendous army of people of this sort is on requisition for the realization of this goal.

8- We should spare no effort to train and educate vicious leaders and cruel commanders in Muslim countries, to bring them into power and thus to pass laws prohibiting obedience to the Shari'at (religious injunctions). We should put them to use, to the extent that they should be subservient enough to do whatever the Ministry (of the Commonwealth) asks them to do, and vice versa. Through them we should be able to impose our wishes on Muslims and Muslim countries by using laws as an enforcement. We should establish a social way of life, an atmosphere wherein obeying the Shari'at will be looked on as a guilt and worshipping as an act of regression. We should trick Muslims into electing their leaders from among non-Muslims. For doing this, we should disguise some of our agents as Islamic authorities and bring them into high positions so that they may execute our wishes.[75]

9- Do your best to prevent the learning of Arabic. Popularize languages other than Arabic, such as Persian, Kurdish, and Pushtu (Pashto). Resuscitate foreign languages in the Arabic countries and popularize the local dialects in order to annihilate literary, eloquent Arabic, which is the language of the Qur'ân and the Sunna.

10- Placing our men around statesmen, we should gradually make them secretaries of these statesmen and through them we should carry out the desires of the Ministry. The easiest way of doing this is the slave trade: First of all we must adequately train the spies we are to send forth in the guise of slaves and concubines. Then we must sell them to the close relatives of Muslim statesmen, for instance, to their children or wives, or to other people liked or respected by them. These slaves, after we have sold them, will gradually apporach the statesmen. Becoming their mothers and governesses, they will encircle Muslim statesmen like a bracelet girding a wrist.

11- Missionary areas must be widened so as to penetrate into all social classes and vocations, especially into such professions as medicine, engineering, and book-keeping. We must open centers of propaganda and publication under such names as churches, schools,

[75] The British were succesful in these endeavours of theirs. They brought their masonic disciples, such as Mustafa Rashîd Pâsha, Alî Pâsha, Fuâd Pâsha, and Tal'at Pâsha, and degenerate people of Armenian or Jewish origin into power. And other masonic men of religion, such as Abdullah Cevdet, Mûsâ Kâzim, and Abduh, were made religious authorities.

hospitals, libraries and charity institutions in the Islamic countries and spread them far and near. We must distribute millions of Christian books free of charge. We must publish the Christian history and intergovernmental law alongside the Islamic history. We must disguise our spies as monks and nuns and place them in churches and monasteries. We must use them as leaders of Christian movements. These people will at the same time detect all the movements and trends in the Islamic world and report to us instantaneously. We must institute an army of Christians who will, under such names as 'professor', 'scientist', and 'researcher', distort and defile the Islamic history, learn all the facts about Muslims' ways, behaviour, and religious principles, and then destory all their books and eradicate the Islamic teachings.

12- We must confuse the minds of the Islamic youth, boys and girls alike, and arouse doubts and hesitations in their minds as to Islam. We must completely strip them of their moral values by means of schools, books, magazines [sports clubs, publications, motion pictures, television], and our own agents trained for this job. It is a prerequisite to open clandestine societies to educate and train Jewish, Christian and other non-Muslim youngsters and use them as decoys to trap the Muslim youngsters.

13- Civil wars and insurrections must be provoked; Muslims must always be struggling with one another as well as against non- Muslims so that their energies will be wasted and improvement and unity will be impossible for them. Their mental dynamisms and financial sources must be annihilated. Young and active ones must be done away with. Their orders must be rendered into terror and anarchy.

14- Their economy must be razed in all areas, their sources of income and agricultural areas must be spoilt, their irrigation channels and lines must be devastated and rivers dried up, the people must be made to hate the performance of namâz and working, and sloth must be made as widespread as possible. Playgrounds must be opened for lazy people. Narcotics and alcoholic spirits must be made common.

[The articles we have cited above were explained very clearly with such aids as maps, pictures and charts.]

I thanked the secretary for giving me a copy of this magnificent document.

After a month's stay in London, I received a message from the Ministry ordering me to go to Iraq to see Muhammad of Najd again. As I was leaving for my mission, the secretary said to me, "Never be negligent about Muhammad of Najd! As it is understood from the reports sent by our spies up until now, Muhammad of Najd is a typical fool very convenient for the realization of our purposes.

"Talk frankly with Muhammad of Najd. Our agents talked with him frankly in Isfahân, and he accepted our wishes on terms. The terms he stipulated are: He would be supported with adequate property and weaponry to protect himself against states and scholars who would certainly attack him upon his announcing his ideas and views. A principality would be established in his country, be it a small one. The Ministry accepted these terms."

I felt as if I were going to fly from joy when I heard this news. I asked the secretary what I was supposed to do about this. His reply was, "The Ministry has devised a subtle scheme for Muhammad of Najd to carry out, as follows:

1- "He is to declare all Muslims as disbelievers and announce that it is halâl to kill them, to seize their property, to violate their chastity, to make their men slaves and their women concubines and to sell them at slave markets."

2- "He is to state that Ka'ba is an idol and therefore it must be demolished.[76] In order to do away with the worship of hajj, he is to provoke tribes to raid groups of hadjis (Muslim pilgrims), to plunder their belongings and to kill them."

3- He is to strive to dissuade Muslims from obeying the Khalîfa. He is to provoke them to revolt against him. He is to prepare armies for this purpose. He is to exploit every opportunity to spread the conviction that it is necessary to fight against the

---

[76] Persons, statues, (or icons) worshipped, offered prostrations to, and looked on as the only authority to provide one's wishes are called 'idols'. Muslims do not offer their prostrations to Ka'ba. Turning towards Ka'ba, they offer their prostrations to Allâhu ta'âlâ. In each prayer of namâz, after performing their prostration towards Ka'ba, they recite the Fâtihâ sûra. It is purported in this sûra, "O Thou, the Unique [only one] Rabb of âlams (universe)! Thee, alone, do we worship. From Thee, alone, do we ask for everything."

notables of Hedjaz and bring disgrace on them.

4- He is to allege that the mausoleums, domes and sacred places in Muslim countries are idols and polytheistic milieus and must therefore be demolished. He is to do his best to produce occasions for insulting Prophet Muhammad, his Khalîfas, and all prominent scholars of madh-habs.

5- "He is to do his utmost to encourage insurrections, oppressions and anarchy in Muslim countries.

6- He is to try to publish a copy of the Qur'ân interpolated with additions and excisions, as is the case with hadîths."[77]

After explaining this six-paragraph scheme, the secretary added, "Do not panic at this huge programme. For our duty is to sow the seeds for annihilating Islam. There will come generations to complete this job. The British government has formed it a habit to be patient and to advance step by step. Wasn't Prophet Muhammad, the performer of the great and bewildering Islamic revolution, a human being after all? And this Muhammad of Najd of ours has promised to accomplish this revolution of ours like his Prophet."

A couple of days later, I took permission from the

---

[77] It would be a very grave slander to assert that there are additions and excisions in the hadîth-i-sherîfs in the well-known and authentic books (of hadîth). A person who has learned how thousands of hadîth scholars compiled hadîth-i-sherîfs could never tell such an abominable lie, nor would he believe lies of this sort.

Minister and the Secretary, bid farewell to my family and friends, and set out for Basra. As I left home my little son said, "Come back soon daddy!" My eyes became wet. I could not conceal my sorrow from my wife. After a tiresome journey I arrived in Basra at night. I went to Abd-ur-Ridâ's home. He was asleep. He was very much pleased when he woke up and saw me. He offered me warm hospitality. I spent the night there. The next morning he said to me, "Muhammad of Najd called on me, left this letter for you, and left." I opened the letter. He wrote he was leaving for his country, Najd, and gave his address there. I at once set out to go there, too. After an extremely onerous journey I arrived there. I found Muhammad of Najd in his home. He had lost a lot of weight. I did not say anything concerning this to him. Afterwards, I learned that he had gotten married.

We decided between us that he was to tell other people that I was his slave and was back from some place he had sent me. He introduced me as such.

I stayed with Muhammad of Najd for two years. We made a programme to announce his call. Eventually I fomented his resolution in 1143 Hijri [A.D. 1730]. Hence by collecting supporters around himself, he insinuated his call by making covert statements to those who were very close to him. Then, day by day, he expanded his call. I put guards around him in order to protect him against his enemies. I gave them as much property and money as they wanted. Whenever the enemies of Muhammad of Najd wanted to attack him, I inspirited and heartened them. As his call spread wider, the number of his adversaries increased. From time to time he attempted to give up his call, especially when he was overwhelmed by the multitude of the attacks made on him. Yet I never left him alone and always encouraged him. I would say to him, "O Muhammad, the Prophet suffered more persecution than you have so far. You know, this is a way of honour. Like any other revolutionist, you would have to endure some difficulty!"

Enemy attack was likely any moment. I therefore hired spies on his adversaries. Whenever his enemies meant harm to him, the spies would report to me and so I would neutralize their harm. Once I was informed that the enemies were to kill him. I immediately took the precautions to thwart their preparations. When the people (around Muhammad of Najd) heard about this plot of their enemies, they began to hate them all the more. They fell into the trap they had laid.

Muhammad of Najd promised me that he would implement all the six articles of the scheme and added, "For the time being I can execute them only partly." He was right in this word of his. At that time it was impossible for him to carry out all of them.

He found it impossible to have Ka'ba demolished. And he gave up the idea of announcing that it (Ka'ba) is an idol. In addition, he refused to publish an interpolated copy of the Qur'ân. Most of his fears in this respect were from the Sherîfs in Mekka and the Istanbul government. He told me that "If we made these two announcements we would be attacked by a powerful army." I accepted his excuse. For he was right. The conditions were not favourable at all.

A couple of years later the Ministry of the Commonwealth managed to cajole Muhammad bin Su'ûd, the Amîr of Der'iyya, into joining our lines. They sent me a messenger to inform me about this and to establish a mutual affection and cooperation between the two Muhammads. For earning Muslims' hearts and trusts, we exploited our Muhammad of Najd religiously, and Muhammad bin Su'ûd politically. It is an historical fact that states based on religion have lived longer and have been more powerful and more imposing.

Thus we continuously became more and more powerful. We made **Der'iyya** city our capital. And we named our new religion the **WAHHÂBÎ** religion. The Ministry supported and reinforced the Wahhâbî government in an underhanded way. The new government bought eleven British officers, very well learned in the Arabic language and desert warfare, under the name of slaves. We prepared our plans in cooperation with these officers. Both Muhammads followed the way we showed them. When we did not receive any orders from the Ministry we made our own decisions.

We all married girls from tribes. We enjoyed the pleasure of a Muslim wife's devotion to her husband. Thus we had stronger relations with tribes. Everything goes well now. Our centralization is becoming more and more vigorous each day. Unless an unexpected adversity takes place, we shall eat the fruit we have prepared. For we have done whatever is necessary and sown the seeds.

Warning

Aperson who reads this book with attention will realize that Islam's arch enemy is the British and will know very well that the Wahhâbî sect, whose votaries have been attacking the Sunnite Muslims all over the world, was founded and is being supported by the British.

This book proves with documentaries that the Wahhâbî sect was founded by British unbelievers with a view to annihilating Islam. We hear that heretics in every country are striving to spread Wahhabism. There are even people who claim that Hempher's confessions are imaginary stories written by others. But they cannot furnish any evidence to prove this claim of theirs.

Those who read Wahhabite books and learn the inner, essential facts about them realize that these confessions are true. Wahhâbîs help demolish Islam. No matter how hard they may try, they will not be able to annihilate the Ahl as-sunna, who are true Muslims, but they themselves will perish, instead. For Allâhu ta'âlâ gives the good news through the eighty-first âyat of Isrâ sûra that the heretics that will appear will be beaten and annihilated by the people of the right way.

Part II

Hüseyin Hilmi Işık

BRITISH ENMITY AGAINST ISLAM

People who read the British spy's confessions given in the first section will have an idea of what the British think about Muslims throughout the world. The following is an account of how British spies have applied the orders they received from the Ministry of the Commonwealth on the world's Muslims and what activities the missionaries have been carrying on.

The British are a conceited and arrogant people. The high value which they attach to themselves and to their own country leaves its place to a symmetrical detestation when it comes to other people and their countries.

According to the British, there are three groups of people on the earth: The first group are the British, who are self-portraited as the most developed beings Allah has ever created in the human form. The second group are the white-coloured Europeans and Americans. These people may also be worthy of respect, as they so generously admit. The third group are the people who have not had the luck of being born in either of the first two groups. They are the sort of creatures between human beings and animals. They are not worthy of respect at all; nor do they deserve such things as freedom, independence or a country. They have been created for living under others' domination, especially that of the British.

Holding such a prejudice about other people, the

British never live among the inhabitants of their colonies. Throughout their colonies there are clubs, casinos, restaurants, baths, and even stores that are open only to British people. Native people cannot enter these places.

French writer Marcelle Perneau, who is famous for his travels to India in the early twentieth century, gives the following account in his **Notes on My Travel to India:**

"I made an appointment with an Indian scholar, who was widely known in Europe, so much so that he had been granted professorship by some universities; we decided to meet in a British club in India. When the Indian arrived, the British did not let him in, disignoring his fame. It was only after I found out what was happening and insisted that I was able to see the Indian in the club."

The British have treated other people with such cruelty as could not be inflicted on animals.

Their biggest colony is India, where they perpetrated savage, sadistic cruelties for years; in the Amritsar city of this country a group of Hindus who had come together for a religious rite did not pay due respect to a British woman missionary. The missionary complained to the British General Dyer. Upon this the general ordered his soldiers to open fire on the people performing their rite. Seven hundred people were killed in ten minutes, and more than a thousand people were wounded. Unsatisfied with this, the general forced the people to walk on their hands and feet like animals for three days. A complaint was filed and reported to London, whereupon the government issued an order for an investigation.

When the inspector sent forth to India for the investigation asked the general for what reason he had ordered his soldiers to open fire on defenceless people, the general answered, "I am the commander here. I make the decisions about the military executions here. I ordered so because I considered it right." When the inspector asked what was the reason for his ordering the people to crawl face downwards, the general answered, "Some Indians crawl face downwards before their gods. I wanted them to know that a British woman is as sacred as a Hindu god, and, therefore, they have to crawl in front of her, too, let alone insulting her." And when the inspector reminded him that the people would have to go out for shopping and other things, the general's answer was, "If these people were human beings they would not crawl on their faces in the streets. They live in adjacent houses with flat roofs. They would walk on their roofs like human beings." These statements of the general's were publicized by the British press and the general was declared a hero. [Dyer, Reginald Edward Harry was born in 1281 [A.D. 1864] and died in London in 1346 [A.D. 1927]. The world's histories mention him as "The famous British general who quelled the riots against the British oppression in Amritsar city by turning the city into a lake of blood on April 13, 1919." When large mass demonstrations against the British were staged all over India, he was discharged from office and retired. However, the British House of Lords decided that his deeds deserved laud and praise, and he must therefore be supported. This fact makes it quite clear how British lords and counts look on other peoples.]

The British apply a different administrative system in their colonies with white and originally European people than the one by which they colonize countries whose people are coloured and aboriginal. The first group are privileged; that is, they are partly autonomous. The second group moan with the pains of cruelty. This second group of their colonies, which they call 'dominions', have self-governing states in their internal affairs, while they are under British domination in their external matters. Examples of these colonies are Canada, Australia, New Zealand, etc.

Matters concerning the colonies have been assigned to two ministries. They are the Ministry of the Commonwealth, and the Ministry of India. The Ministry of the Commonwealth is presided over by **Secretary of State for the Colonial Department.** This secretary (or minister) has two councillors and four assistants. One of the councilors is chosen from among the House of Commons. The other councilor and the assistants are in office permanently. Change of power will not cause them to lose their office. One of the four assistants are in charge of matters concerning Canada, Australia, and some islands, another one is responsible for Southern Africa, a third one governs Eastern and Western Africa, and the last one has been assigned to India.

Based on a fetid foundation, a mixture of hostility against Islam, despotism, trickery and turpitude, the British Empire formerly called itself a state on which "the sun never sets". Such countries as Canada, South Africa, Fiji, the Pacific Islands, Papua, Tonga, Australia, the British Baluchistan, Burma, Aden, Somali, Borneo, Brunei, Sarawak, India, Pakistan, Bangladesh, Malaysia, Indonesia, Hong-Kong, a part of China, Cyprus, Malta, (and in 1300 [A.D. 1882]) Egypt, Sudan, Niger, Nigeria, Kenya, Uganda, Zimbabwe, Zambia, Malawi, Bahamas, Grenada, Guiana (Guyana), Bostwana, Gambia, Ghana, Sierra Leone, Tanzania, and Singapore were brought under the British sway. These countries of the world lost their religions, languages, customs and traditions. In addition, their sources and resources were exploited by the Britsh.

At the end of their invasions in the nineteenth century, the Empire took possession of approximately one-fourth of the earth's surface, colonizing more than one-fourth of the earth's population.

India was the most significant, the most outstanding of the British colonies. It was India's tremendous population of over three hundred million [well over seven hundred million as of today] and its inexhaustible natural wealths that earned the British their universal domination. In the First World War alone, Britain utilized one and a half million of India's population as fighting soldiers and one billion rupees of its treasury as ready money. They used most of these assets in smashing the Ottoman Empire. In peace time as well, it was India that helped Britain's stupendous industries to survive and sustained the British economy and finance. There were two reasons for India's being an incomparably important colony: First, India was a country where Islam, which the British considered to be the greatest hindrance to their exploiting the whole world, was widespread, and Muslims were in the ascendant in this country. Second, India's natural riches.

In order to keep India under their domination, the British mounted offensives on all the Muslim countries that had transport links with India, sowed seeds of mischief and instigation, set brothers against one another, took these countries under their domination, and transported all their natural riches and national wealth back to their own country.

The perfidious character inherent in the nature of the British policy proves itself in that they meticulously followed the movements in the Ottoman Empire, set the Ottomans on a war with the Russians by using all sorts of political stratagems, and thus put them into a position wherefore it would be impossible for them to offer any help to India.

The European pioneers of India are the Portuguese. Landing in the port city named Calcutta in India's coastal Malabar region in 904 [A.D. 1498], the Portuguese engaged in trade and took possession of India's trade business, only to lose it to the Dutch some time later. Those who snatched India's trade from the Ducth were the French. It was not long after that, however, that these people confronted with the British.

As it is related in the book **As-Sawrat-ul-Hindiyya,** (which means **'the Indian Revolution'**), written by Allâma Muhammad Fadl-i-Haqq Khayr-âbâdî, one of India's great Islamic scholars, and in its commentary entitled **Al-yawâkît-ul-mihriyya,** it was in the year

1008 [A.D. 1600] when the British first managed to take Akbar Shâh's permission to open trade centers in Calcutta, India. The same year Queen Elizabeth I sanctioned the regulations for the **East Indian** Campaign. In accordance with these regulations, the campaign was granted permission to recruit soldiers in Britain, to arm them for its own use, to establish a fleet of its own, and to organize military and commercial expeditions to India.

They bought land in Calcutta in the time of Shâh-i-'Âlam I.[78] They brought soldiers with the pretext of protecting their land. Akbar Shâh was a corrupt person in credal matters. He held all religions equal. In fact, he convened scholars from various religions and attempted to establish a common, universal religion, a mixture of all religions, and made an official announcement of this new religion, which he named **Dîn-i-ilâhî** (Divine Religion), in 990 [A.D. 1582]. From that time up until his death, respect for Islamic scholars continuously decreased all over India, especially in the palace, and people who tended towards Akbar Shâh's religion were esteemed highly. It was during those days when the British entered India. In return for their successful medical treatment of Sultân Farrûh Sîr Shâh in 1126 [A.D. 1714], they were awarded the privilege of buying land anywhere they liked throughout India. After Shâh-i-'Âlam II mounted the throne 1174 [A.D. 1760], they extended their domination from Bengal to Central India and Racasthan. They aroused mischief and tumults everywhere in India. In 1218 [A.D. 1803] the British eventually managed to take Shâh-i-'Âlam II completely

---

[78] Shâh-i-'Âlam bin Alamgîr passed away in 1124 [C.E. 1712].

under their authority. The orders which they announced
from Delhi were now being issued in the name of the
Shâh. It did not take them long to equalize the powers
of the British governor general with those of Shâh-i-
'Âlam II. They deleted the names of the Muslim Indian
emperors from the Indian monetary coins. In 1253
[C.E. 1837] Bahâdir Shâh II became the emperor. He
could not stand the British oppressions long and,
encouraged by the army and the people, commenced a
great insurrection against the British in 1274 [A.D.
1857]. Thus, he managed to have money coined bearing
his name and to have the khutba given with his name
mentioned in it, yet the British reaction to this was
extremely vehement and cruel. Entering Delhi, the
British soldiers made havoc of the city, ransacked
houses and shops, and pillaged whatever they found in
the name of property and money. They put all Muslims
to the sword, regardless of whether they were young or
old, male or female, adult or infant. It was such a
massive destruction that the people could not even find
any water to drink.

One of the commanders of Bahâdir Shâh II, a
general named Baht Khân, persuaded the Sultan to
withdraw his army. However, another commander
named Mirzâ Ilâhî Bakhsh, in an effort to ingratiate
himself with the British, misled Bahâdir Shâh, saying
that if he left his army and surrendered he would be
able to convince the British that he was innocent and
had been forced to preside over the insurrection and
thus would be forgiven by the British. So Bahâdir Shâh
left the main body of his retreating army and took
asylum in Humâyûn Shâh's mausoleum, ten kilometres
from a place called Qal'a-i-Muallâ within Delhi.

A traitor named Rajab Alî betrayed the Emperor to a British priest named Hudson, who was notorious for immoral and maladroit acts and was serving as an intelligence officer in the British army. This man, in his turn, reported the situation to General Wilson, the then Army Commander, and asked for his help to arrest the Emperor. When Wilson answered that he did not have any mercenaries to lend him, Hudson suggested that he could do this job with a few men, advising that the Emperor must be given the guarantee that he and his family would not be harmed if he surrendered. At first Wilson refused this suggestion, but after a while he agreed. Upon this Hudson, taking ninety men with him, went to Humâyûn Shâh's mausoleum and assured the Emperor that no harm would be inflicted on him, his sons and wife. Falling for the priets's promise, Bahâdir Shâh surrendered. The Emperor had two sons and a grandson who had not surrendered yet. So Hudson set about to arrest them. Yet they had so many guards that it was impossible to arrest them. Therefore he took General Wilson's permission to give them the guarantee that they would not be harmed if they surrendered. Sending various messengers to the Emperor's two sons and grandson, Hudson, the villain, assured them that they would not be harmed. These people also were taken in by the priest's lies and surrendered. As soon as Hudson arrested the Emperor's two sons and grandson, by having recourse to a policy and stratagem peculiar to the British, he cast them into chains.

As the Shâh's two sons and grandson were being taken to Delhi with their hands tied, Hudson had the young princes stripped of their clothes and he martyred them himself by firing bullets into their chests. He drank from their blood. He had the corpses of these young martyrs hung by the fortress gate in order to intimidate the people. The following day he sent their heads to the British governor general Henry Bernard. Then, he had a bowl of soup made from the martyrs' flesh and sent it to the Shâh and his spouse. Being very hungry, they hastily put some into their mouths. Yet, although they did not know what kind of meat it was, they could not chew it or swallow it. Instead, they vomited and put the soup dishes on the floor. The villian named Hudson said, "Why don't you eat it. It is delicious soup. I had it cooked from your sons' flesh."

In 1275 [A.D. 1858] Bahâdir Shâh II was dethroned and was subjected to a judicial trial for the crime of causing rebellion and massacre of Europeans. On March 29, he was sentenced to life imprisonment and was banished to Indo-China [Rangoon]. It was during November of 1279 [A.D. 1862] that this last Sultan of the Islamic Ghurghânî Empire, Bahâdir Shâh, passed away in a dungeon far from his country. On the other hand, Allâma (Muhammad) Fadl-i-Haqq was martyred by the British in a dungeon on the Andaman Islands in 1278 [C.E. 1861].

During the Ottoman-Russian War, in 1294 [C.E. 1877], the British declared India a British dependency. By submerging the Ottoman Empire into this war, Midhat Pâsha, a registered member of the notorious Scotch Masonic Lodge, orchestrated the worst of the damage he had inflicted on the Islamic religion. His having martyred Sultân Abd-ul-'Azîz Khân was another favour he did for the British. The British had trained special agents and had them appointed to high ranking positions in the Ottoman government. These statesmen were Ottoman in name but British in mind and speech. Mustafa Rashîd Pâsha, the most infamous of these men, had been in office as the last Grand Vizier only six days when he congratulated the British for the Delhi massacre they perpetrated on the Muslims of India on 28 Oct. 1857. Earlier than that, the British had asked permission from the Ottomans to use the Egyptian route for the dispatch of the British soldiers coming from Britain to suppress the Muslims who had revolted against the British cruelty in India. The permission had been provided by the masonic agents.

The British not only prevented the opening of new schools in India, but they also closed all the madrasas and the primary schools which were the foundations and the most salient symbols of the Islamic Sharî'at, and they martyred all the scholars and religious authorities who could have led the people. At this point we consider it appropriate to relate a real story that a friend of ours told us when he was back from his travels to India and Pakistan in 1391 [A.D. 1971].

"After visiting the graves of the Awliyâ, such as Imâm-i- Rabbânî and others 'qaddas-Allâhu sirrah' in Serhend city, I went to Pâniput city, and thence to Delhi. Performing the Friday prayer in the biggest mosque in Pâniput. I went to the imâm's house upon his invitation. On the way I saw a huge door locked with a chain with thick rings. The inscription on the door said it had been a primary school. I asked the imâm why it was locked. The imâm said, 'It has been closed since 1367 [A.D. 1947]. The British provoked the Hindus against the Muslims and caused a massacre of all the Muslims, women, men, children and old people, all of them. This school has been closed since that day. This chain and the lock remind us of the British cruelty. We are emigrants who came and settled here afterwards.' "

The British did away with all the Islamic scholars, Islamic books, and Islamic schools, a practice which they applied to all the Islamic countries. Thus they brought up young generations totally unaware of the religion.

The notorious British Lord Macauley, as soon as he arrived in Calcutta in 1834, prohibited all sorts of Arabic and Persian publications and ordered that the ones that were already in the process of printing should be stopped, and this attitude of his earned him a great deal of acclamation from his British colleagues. This oppression was assiduously carried on in places with a Muslim majority, especially in Bengal.

While closing the Islamic madrasas in India on the one hand, the British opened one hundred and sixty-five colleges, eight of which were for girls, on the other hand. The students educated in these colleges were brainwashed and were made hostile towards their fathers' religion, towards their own ancestors. Two-thirds of the British army that perpetrated the aforesaid cruelties and savageries in India was made up of the native people who had been brainwashed, made hostile against their own nation, Christianized, or hired.

The laws that were enacted in 1249 [C.E. 1833] served the expansion of the missionary activities and the consolidation of the Protestant organization in India. Before this spreading of missionary activities and India's being fully under British domination, the British were respectful of the Muslims' religious belief; they would have cannons fired to celebrate the Muslims' holy days, offer them help for the restoration of their mosques and other places of worship, and even join services in the pious foundations pertaining to mosques, convents, shrines and madrasas. The imperative messages arriving from Britain in 1833 and 1838 prohibited the British from activities of this sort. As these facts show clearly, the policy employed by the British in their attacks on the Islamic religion is based on deceiving the world's Muslims by first pretending to be friendly and helpful and by spreading the impression far and wide that they love Muslims and serve Islam, and then, after attaining this subsidiary goal, annihilating gradually and insidiously all the Islamic essentials, books, schools, and scholars. This double-faced policy of theirs has done the worst harm to Muslims and all but exterminated Islam. Later on, they increased their efforts to have English adopted as the official language and bring up Christianized new generations from the native people. To this end they opened schools thoroughly under the control of the missionaries. In fact, the British Prime Minister Lord Palmerston and many other British Lords said that "God hath given India to the British so that the Indian people might enjoy the blessings of Christianity."

Lord Macauley spent his utmost energy and support for constituting in India a British nation who were Indian in blood and colour and British in inclinations, thoughts, belief, moral values, and mental capacity.

Therefore, the schools opened by the missionaries allotted very much importance and time in their curricula to the teaching of the English language and literature and Christianity. Scientific knowledge, (such as mathematics, physics, chemistry, etc.), was totally disignored. Thus a number of Christianized people who knew nothing but the English language and literature were educated and produced. Then these people were employed in the civil service.

It being an Islamic rule that a Muslim who abandons his faith will become an apostate, while Hindus considered those who turn away from Hinduism irreligious, people who were Christianized could not inherit property from their parents. In order to eliminate this rule, the missionaries passed a law, which was first enacted in Bengal, in 1832, and then promulgated all over India, in 1850, thus making it possible for the Christianized native apostates and renegades to have a share from their parents' inheritance. For this reason, Indians called the British schools in India **Satanic Registers.** [In India and in the Ottoman Empire official bureaus and institutions were called Defter (Register).] French writer Marcelle Permeau visited India in 1344 [A.D. 1925] and published a book when he returned. He says in this book of his, "Calcutta, India's primary city, was in such a miserable state that the poverty-stricken purlieus around Paris and London would fall far short of exemplifying. People and animals living together in cottages, children crying, ill people moaning. Beside them you see people utterly enervated from continuous use of alcohol and drugs, sprawling on the ground in a manner no different from dead people. Watching these exceedingly hungry, miserable, weak and exhausted people, one cannot help asking oneself what on earth these people could do.

"Clouds of people are scudding towards factories, and how much of their profits are these factories paying these people? Needs, difficulties, infectious diseases, alcohol and drugs are destroying, annihilating the already enervated, defenceless people. Nowhere else on earth has human life been treated with such shameless indifference as it is here. No work, no toil is considered to be hard or unhealthy here. It is not a problem if a worker dies. Another one will take his place. The only concern for the British here is how to increase the production rates and how to earn more and more money."

Williams Jennings Bryan, a former U.S. Foreign Secretary, confirms with evidences that the British government is more cruel and baser than Russia; the statements he makes in his book **British Domination in India** can be paraphrased as follows: "The British, who claim to have bestowed welfare and happiness on the living of the Indian people, sent millions of Indians to their graves. This nation (the British), who boast everywhere that they instituted law courts and disciplinary forces, robbed India to the core through a political embezzlement. 'Robbery' may sound somewhat too tough a term, yet no other word could depict the British atrocity more explicitly.

"The conscience of the British people, who claim to be Christians, is not willing to hear the Indian Muslims' call for help."

Mister Hodbert Keombtun says in his book **Life of the Indian,** "The Indian is tormented by his master [the British], yet he continues to work and serve till he loses everything he has, till he dies."

The Indian Muslim workers being employed in the other British colonies were even under worse conditions. In 1834 the British industrialists began to employ Indian workers instead of African natives. Thousands of Muslims were transported from India to South African colonies. The position of these workers, who were called **coolies,** was worse than that of slaves. They were bound by a contract called **indentured labour.** According to this contract, the coolie would be indentured for five years. During this period he could not leave his work or get married; he would have to work day and night under continuous whipping. In addition, he was liable to a taxation of three British gold coins yearly. "These facts were announced all over the world through publications such as **Labour in India, Post-Lecturer in the University of New York.**"

Ghandi, a widely known Indian Ruler, received his education in Britain and returned to India. He was the son of a Christianized Indian. In fact, his father was the Archbishop of Porbandar city. When in 1311 [A.D. 1893] he was sent by a British company in India to South Africa and witnessed the heavy conditions the Indians were being employed under and the barbarous treatment they were being subjected to, he put up a struggle against the British. Although he was the son of a person brought up and even Christianized by the British, he could not bear the sight of this British cruelty and savagery. This was his first step towards the movement that would later earn him his renown.

The basis of the policy which the British have followed throughout the Muslim world consists of this three-word slogan: "Break, dominate, and destroy their faith."

They have not hesitated to fulfil all the requirements of this policy, whatsoever.

The first thing they did in India was to find the people who would serve them. Using these people, they slowly lit the fire of mischief. The people most suitable for this purpose were the Hindus living under Muslims' domination; so they used these people. The Hindus were leading a peaceful life under the equitable ruling of the Muslims, when the British approached them and gradually imbued them with the thought that Hindus were the real owners of India, that Muslims had been killing the Hindu gods in the name of religious sacrifice, and that this practice should soon be put an end to. The Hindus were on the British side now. They employed some of them as mercenaries. Thus the Hindu nescience and the British hostility against Islam and avarice for money were brought together to carry out Queen Elizabeth's advice for the formation of an army. Discord was sown between the Muslim governors and the Hindu maharajahs. In the meantime, from amongst the Muslims, people slack in their faith were hired.

The British Sir Lord Strachey, who served as the regent on several occasions and who was a member of the (Indian Organization), states about the Muslim-Hindu enmity, "Anything that will be done in order to dominate or sow discord is compatible with our government's policy. The greater support for our policy in India is the co-existence of two autonomous societies who are hostile to each other." Aggravating this hostility, the British supported the Hindus continuously from 1164 [A.D. 1750] until 1287 [A.D. 1870], and joined them in all the massacres of Muslims they perpetrated.

Commencing in 1858, the Muslim-Hindu conflicts grew wider and wider. The British would provoke the Hindus against the Muslims and then sit and enjoy the fights as the Hindus attacked. Not a single year passed without bloody events and mischievous tumults that broke out upon the killing of a cow as a religious sacrifice and which resulted in the massacre of hundreds, nay, thousands of Muslims. In order to kindle the mischief from both ends, they, on the one hand, spread among the Muslims the belief that killing one cow as a sacrifice would be more pious than killing seven sheep, and, on the other hand, they rumoured among the Hindus that rescuing their bovine gods from death would earn them a lot of rewards in the next world. This mischief of theirs continued after their withdrawal from India. We would like to exemplify this fact by relating an event written in a magazine entitled **Ittilâ'at,** which was published in Iran in the time of its Prime Minister Musaddiq.

On a day of Qurbân[79] two bearded Muslims wearing turbans and long robes bought a cow to kill as a

---

[79] One of the Muslims' holy days on which they slaughter a sheep, a cow, or a camel as a religious sacrifice.

sacrifice. As they were passing a Hindu quarter on their way home, a Hindu stopped them to ask them what they were going to do with the cow. When they said they were going to kill it as a sacrifice, the Hindu began to shout, "Hey, people! Help! These men are going to sacrifice our god." And the two Muslims also shouted, "O Muslims! Help! These men are going to seize our sacrifice." Hindus and Muslims gathered around the place and began to fight by using sticks and knives. Hundreds of Muslims were killed. Later, however, the two people who had been taking the cow through the Hindu quarter were seen disappearing into the British embassy. This comes to mean that this event was provoked by the British. The correspondent who relates this event adds, "We know how you spoiled Muslims' day of Qurbân." With tricks of this sort and innumerable other types of cruelty they tried to destroy Muslims.

Later on, when they saw that the Hindus were gradually rising against them, they began, by 1287 [A.D. 1870], to support the Muslims against the Hindus.

There appeared strange people who bore Muslim names yet who were hostile against the Ahl as-sunna, said that it was not fard to make Jihâd with the sword, said 'halâl' about what Islam has prescribed to be harâm, and attempted to change Islam's principles of belief. Sir Sayyed Ahmad, Ghulâm Ahmad Qâdiyânî, Abdullah Ghaznawî, Ismâ'îl-i-Dahlawî, Nazîr Huseyn Dahlawî, Siddiq Hasan Khân Pehûpâlî, Rashîd Ahmad Kenkuhî, Wahîd uz-zamân Haydar Âbâdî, Ashraf Alî Tahânawî, and Muhammad Is-haq, who was Shâh Abd-ul-azîz's grandson, were only a few of these people.

Supporting these people, the British caused the appearance of other new sects. They strove to make Muslims follow these sects.

The most notorious of these sects was the **Qâdiyânî,** which appeared in 1296 [A.D. 1879]. Its founder, Ghulâm Ahmad, said it was not fard (Islam's commandment) to make Jihâd (Holy War) by means of weaponry and that Jihâd which was fard was advice. So did the British spy Hempher say to Muhammad of Najd.

Ghulâm Ahmad was a heretic belonging to the Ismâ'îlî group. He died in 1326 [C.E. 1908]. The British hired him for a considerable sum of money. Formerly he claimed to be a Mujaddîd; then he promoted his claim to being the promised Mahdî; his next step was to assert that he was Jesus the Messiah. Finally, he announced that he was a Prophet and had been revealed a new religion. He called the people he had managed to deceive his 'ummat', asserted that many âyats had foretold of him and that he displayed more miracles than had any other Prophet. He alleged that those who would not believe him were unbelievers. His sect spread among the ignorant people in Punjab and Bombay. The Qâdiyânî sect is still spreading under the name **Ahmadiyya** movement in Europe and America.

The Sunnî Muslims said that it was fard to perform Jihâd through arms and that it was heresy to serve the British. Muslims who preached or advised this were punished vehemently and mostly killed. The Sunnite books were gathered and destroyed.

Islamic scholars who could not be hired or would not serve the British purposes would be isolated from the Muslim community. They would not be executed lest they should become famous, but they would be given life imprisonment in the notorious dungeons on the Andaman Islands. All the Islamic scholars arrested throughout India on the pretext that they had been collaborating with the rebels during the revolution were sent to the same dungeons. [Likewise, when they invaded Istanbul after World War I, they banished the Ottoman Pâshas and scholars to Malta Island.]

In order that the Muslims should not notice their grudge against Islam, they received fatwâs defining India as a Dâr-ul-islâm and not as a Dâr-ul-harb, and spread these fatwâs everywhere.

The hypocrites whom they had trained and named scholars propagated the impression that the Ottoman Sultans were not Khalîfas, that caliphate belonged to the Qoureishis by right, that the Ottoman Sultans had taken possession of caliphate by force and therefore should not be obeyed.

[The hadîth-i-sherîf, **"The Khalîfa shall be from the Qoureish tribe,** (from their descendants)," means, "If there are Qoureishis, [e.g. sayyids], among the people who deserve to be and fulfil the conditions for being the Khalîfa, you should prefer (one of) these people." If there is not such a person, someone else should be elected. If a person has not been elected the Khalîfa, or has refused to obey the elected Khalîfa and has seized power by using force or violence, this person will have to be obeyed. There can be only one Khalîfa on the earth. All Muslims have to obey him.]

In order to extirpate religious teachings and demolish Islam from within, they opened a madrasa for the teaching of Islamic knowledge and an Islamic university in Aligarh. In these schools they educated religious men who were unaware of religion and hostile to Islam. These people caused great harms to Islam. A group of these people were chosen, sent to Britain, trained in such a way as to demolish Islam from within, and brought to government positions where they would preside over Muslims. Ayyub Khân, who was made Pakistan's president in place of M. Jinnah, was one of them.

Although the British seem to have been one of the winners of the Second World War, actually they lost the war. In fact, Britain, "a country where the sun never sets," as the British called their land, became "a country where the sun never rises" after the war. Having lost all its colonies, it was like a plucked hen.

Ali Jinnah, who was made Pakistan's president, was a Shiite and a British fan. When he died in 1367 [A.D. 1948] Ayyub Khân, a freemason, seized power by staging a coup d'etat. Also Yahyâ Khân, who took this disbeliever's place, was a bigoted Shiite. When he was defeated in the war between Pakistan and India in early 1392 [C.E. 1972], he lost control of Eastern Pakistan and was imprisoned. In 1971 Yahyâ Khân handed the government over to Zulfikâr Ali Bhutto, who was another British agent educated and trained in Britain. In 1974, the order that he gave for the killing of his adversaries cost him his own execution.

Ziya-ul-Haqq, who took power by casting out Zülfikâr Ali Bhutto, was keen enough to perceive the enemies' plans to destroy Islam and annihilate Muslims; he would not carry out their desires. He endeavoured for his country's improvement in science, technology and arts. Knowing very well that Islam is the only source of welfare and prosperity for individuals, for families, for the society, and for the whole nation, he was thinking of making laws compatible with the Sharî'at. He decided to refer this question to his people. A referandum was held and the people voted for the proposal.

The British villains did their masters another service by assassinating Ziya-ul-Haqq and all his suite. Some time later Ali Bhutto's daughter became prime minister and set free all the villains who had been imprisoned for various crimes against the State, the people, and Islam. She appointed them to high adminisitrative positions. Tumults and conflicts commenced in Pakistan. This state of affairs was what the British desired.

After the First and Second World Wars, in many countries people who would carry out the British plans and protect the British interests were brought to high positions by the British. These countries have had their own national anthems, national flags, and presidents, yet they have never attained religious freedom.

For the last three centuries, any sort of treason committed against the Turkish and Islamic worlds has had the British plotters at its root.

They demolished the Ottoman Empire and

established twenty- three big and small states on its lands. Their purpose in doing this was to hinder Muslims from establishing a powerful and great state.

They always instigated hostilities and wars among countries said to be Islamic countries. For instance, they made the nine- percent Nusayrîs dominant in Syria, where the Sunnîs hold a majority. In 1982 the armed forces attacked the cities Hama and Humus, devastating the two cities and bombing the unarmed, defenceless Sunnî Muslims.

They killed true Sunnî scholars, destroyed Islamic books, including copies of Qur'ân al-kerîm. Instead of these Islamic scholars, they brought religiously ignorant, heretical people they had schooled. Of these people:

Jamâladdîn Afghânî was born in Afghanistan in 1254 [A.D. 1838]. He read philosophy books. He spied on Afghanistan for the Russians. He went to Egypt, where he became a freemason and was appointed the chief of the masonic lodge. Adip Is-haq of Egypt states in his book **Ed-durer** that he was the chief of Cairo masonic lodge. It is stated as follows in the hundred and twenty- seventh page of the book **Les Franço-Maçons,** which was printed in France in 1960: "Jamâladdîn Afghânî was appointed chief of the masonic lodges founded in Egypt, and he was succeeded by Muhammad Abdoh. They provided a great deal of help in the spreading of freemasonry among Muslims."

Alî Pâsha, a five-time Grand Vizier during the reigns of Sultân Abd-ul-Majîd and Sultân Abd-ul-'Azîz, was a freemason affiliated with the British lodge. He invited Afghânî to Istanbul. He gave him some duties. The time's Istanbul University Rector, Hasan Tahsin, who had been declared a heretic through a fatwâ, had Afghânî deliver speeches. Hasan Tahsin had, in his turn, been trained by the Grand Vizier Mustafa Rashîd Pâsha, an affiliated member of the British masonic lodge. Afghânî strove to spread his heretical ideas far and near. Hasan Fehmi Efendi, the time's Shaikh-ul-islâm, confuted Afghânî and proved that he was an ignorant heretic; hence, Alî Pâsha had to expel him from Istanbul. This time he tried to promulgate his ideas of revolution and religious reformation in Egypt. He pretended to support the plotters of **A'râbî Pâsha** against the British. He made friends with Muhammad Abdoh, who was the Muftî of Egypt in those days. He corrupted him with his ideas of making reforms in Islam. Supported by masonic lodges, he began to issue a periodical in Paris and London. Then he went to Iran. He would not behave properly there, either. Consequently, he was fastened with chains and left somewhere on the Ottoman border. Freed somehow, he went to Baghdad, and thence to London, where he wrote articles castigating Iran. Then he went back to Istanbul and used religion as a means for political ends by cooperating with the Bahâîs in Iran.

The most notorious of the victims who fell for Jamâladdîn Afghânî's propagations intended to demolish Islam from within under the cloak of a religious man, was **Muhammad Abdoh,** born in Egypt in 1265 [A.D. 1849], and died there in 1323 [C.E. 1905]. Spending a part of his life in Beirut, he left for Paris, where he joined Jamâladdîn Afghânî's activities prescribed by masonic lodges. They began to issue a periodical named **Al-urwat-ul-Wuthqâ.** Then he came back to Beirut and Egypt, endeavouring to carry out in these places the decisions made by the Paris masonic lodge. Backed by the British, he became the Muftî of Cairo and assumed an offensive attitude towards the Ahl as- sunna. The first step he took in this way was to defile and spoil the curricula in the Jâmi'ul az-har madrasa, thus hindering the teaching of valuable religious lore to the younger generation. He had the lessons being taught at the university level abrogated and put into their curricula the teaching of books that were currently being taught in the secondary level. Stripping the schools of their capacity as places of knowledge on the one hand, he, on the other hand, vituperated the Islamic scholars, pledged that these scholars hindered the teaching of scientific knowledge, and claimed that he would enrich Islam by adding this knowledge to it. He wrote a book entitled **Islam and Christianity,** in which he says, "All religions are the same. They are different only in their outward appearance. Jews, Christians and Muslims should support one another." In a letter he wrote to a priest in London, he says, "I hope to see the two great religions, Islam and Christianity, hand-in-hand, embracing each other. Then the Torah and the Bible and the Koran will become books supporting one another, being read everywhere, and respected by every nation." He adds that he is looking forward to seeing Muslims read the Torah and the Bible.

In his interpretation of Qur'ân al-kerîm, which he wrote in cooperation with **Shaltut,** the director of Jâmi'ul az-har, he gives the fatwâ stating that bank interest is permissible. Later on, fearing that this might incur the wrath of Muslims, he pretended to have withdrawn from this opinion.

Hannâ Abû Râshid, president of the masonic lodges in Beirut, makes the following acknowledgement in the hundred and ninety- seventh page of his book **Dâira-tul-ma'ârif-ul-masoniyya,** which he published in 1381 [A.D. 1961]: "Jamâladdîn Afghânî was the chief of the masonic lodge in Egypt. The lodge had nearly three hundred members, most of them were scholars and statesmen. After him Muhammad Abdoh, the imâm, the master, became the chief. Abdoh was a great freemason. No one could deny the fact that he promoted the masonic spirit all over the Arabic countries."

Another most notorious disbeliver whom the British propagate as an Islamic scholar all over India is Sir Sayyed Ahmad Khân. He was born in Delhi in 1234 [A.D. 1818]. His father had migrated to India during the reign of Akbar Shâh. In 1837 he began to work as a secretary for his paternal uncle, a judge at a British law court in Delhi. He was made a judge in 1841 and was promoted to a higher judgeship in 1855.

Another so-called religious man educated by the British in India is Hamîdullah. He was born in 1326 [A.D. 1908] in Haydarâbâd, where the Ismâ'îlî group were the majority. He was brought up in the Ismâ'îlî group and, therefore, as a fanatical adversary of the Ahl as-sunna. He is a member of the research institution called CNRS in Paris. He strives to introduce Muhammad 'alaihis-salâm' as the Prophet for Muslims only.

In their war to annihilate Islam, the most effective weapon the British used for deceiving Muslims zealous for serving their country and nation was the method of propagating that Islam should be adapted to time, modernized and restored to its original purity, which again was intended to establish an irreligious society. The Shaikh-ul-islâm Mustafa Sabri Efendi, a great Islamic savant, was one of the people who perceived this very well. By stating, "To abrogate the madh-habs means to build a bridge leading to irreligiousness," he elucidated what their real purposes were.

The British and the other enemies of Islam endeavoured assiduously to corrupt the dervish convents and paths of Tasawwuf. They strove hard to annihilate Ikhlâs,which is the third component of the Sharî'at. The superior leaders of Tasawwuf never busied themselves with politics, nor would they expect any worldly advantages from anybody. Most of those great people were profoundly learned mujtahids. For, 'tasawwuf' means to follow the way guided by Muhammad 'alaihis-salâm'. In other words, it means to strictly observe the Sharî'at in whatever one says or does, in everything. However, for a long time, ignorant, sinful people, and even foreign agents, in order to attain their vile goals, have instituted diverse guilds by using the names of great men of Tasawwuf, and thus caused the Islamic religion and its Sharî'at to collapse, to deteriorate. Dhikr, (for instance), means to remember Allâhu ta'âlâ. This is essentially the heart's business. Dhikr purifies the heart of any sort of love except that of Allâhu ta'âlâ, such as love of the world or of other creatures, and thus love of Allah settles firmly in the heart. It is not dhikr for a number of people, men and women, to come together and articulate some strange sounds in the name of dhikr. The way followed by those superior men of religion, by the As-hâb-i-kirâm, has already been forgotten. Ahmad Ibni Taymiyya, a heretic without a certain Madhhab and an enemy of Tasawwuf, was declared an Islamic scholar. A new sect, namely **Wahhâbîism**, was established to follow in his wake. With British support and through Wahhâbî centers that they founded the worldover and called **Râbita-t-ul 'âlam-il-islâmî**, books spreading Wahhâbîism were published in all countries. The huge buildings that they constructed in every country were hung with signs saying: 'Ibni Taymiyya Madrasa'. A mixture of the heretical ideas in Ibni Taymiyya's books and the lies fibbed by the British spy named Hempher was called **Wahhâbîism**. Scholars of Ahl as-sunnat, true Muslims, wrote many books informing that Ibni Taymiya's books are heretical. One of those books is entitled **al-Maqâlât-us-sunniyya fî kashf-i-dalâlât-i-Ahmad Ibni Taymiyya**, by Shaikh 'Abd-ur-Rahmân 'Abdullah bin Muhammad Harrî, a Somalian scholar. That scholar was born in Harar, Somalia, (in Ethiopia as of today,) in 1339 [1920 A.D.]. His book was printed and published in Beirut in 1414 [1994 A.D.]. The book provides a detailed account of the scholars who refuted Ibni Taymiyya and also of the valuable books written by those scholars. Enmity against Tasawwuf is the common villainy of all the heretical sects called Wahhâbîism, Lâ-madhhabîism, Reformism, Salafiyya, Qâdiyânî Movement, Mawdûdîism, and Tablîgh-i-jamâ'at, all of which were established and organized by British plotters.

Enemies of Islam, particularly the British, employed all sorts of methods to retard Muslims in science and technology. Muslims were hampered from trade and arts. Atrocities such as alcoholic spirits, indecencies, revels and gambling were encouraged and popularized in order to spoil the beautiful moral qualities existent in Islamic countries and to annihilate Islamic civilizations. Byzantine, Armenian and other non-Muslim women were employed as agents for depraving people. Young girls were lured into losing their chastity by means of resplendent decoys, such as fashion houses, dance courses, and schools for training mannequins and actresses. Muslim parents still do have very much to do in this respect. They have to be wide awake so as not to let their children fall into the traps set by these impious people.

Towards its declining years, the Ottoman Empire sent students and statesmen out to Europe. Some of these students and statesmen were persuaded into joining masonic lodges. Those who were to learn science and technology were taught techniques for demolishing Islam and the Ottoman Empire. Of these people who did the greatest harm to the Empire and to Muslims was Mustafâ Rashîd Pâsha. His stay in London was entirely appropriated to disciplining him as an avowed and insidious enemy of Islam. He cooperated with the Scottish masonic lodges. It was too late when the Sultân, Mahmûd Khân, took heed of Mustafâ Rashîd Pâsha's treacherous acts and ordered that he be executed; for the remainder of his lifetime was not long enough for him to have his order carried out. After the Sultân's passing away, Mustafâ Rashîd Pâsha and his colleagues returned to Istanbul and did Islam and

Muslims the severest harm they had ever suffered.

Abd-ul-majîd Khân, who became the Pâdishâh in 1255 [A.D. 1839], was in his eighteenth year yet. He was too young and quite inexperienced. Nor did any of the scholars around him warn him. It was this state that caused the deplorable turning point in the Ottoman history and brought the whole Empire to a **declining rhythm** from which it could never recover. The gullible, pure- hearted young Emperor fell for the cajolery of the British, the formidable and insidious enemies of Islam, and appointed the ignoramuses trained by the Scottish masons to administrative positions. He was too immature to sense their policy of demolishing the State from within. And there was no one to caution him. Lord Rading, a cunning member of the **Scottish Masonic Organization,** which had been established in Britain with a view to demolishing Islam, was sent to Istanbul as the British ambassador. With blandishing statements such as, "If you would appoint this cultured and successful vizier as Grand Vizier, all the disagreements between the British Empire and your great Empire would be solved, and the great Ottoman Empire would make progress in economic, social and military areas," he managed to persuade the Khalîfa.

As soon as Rashîd Pâsha took possession of the position of Grand Vizier in 1262 [A.D. 1846], he began to open masonic lodges in large cities, using as a basis for his move the so-called law of **Tanzîmât** [Reorganization], which he had prepared in coordination with Lord Rading as he was Foreign Minister in 1253 and officially promulgated in 1255. Homes of espionage and treason began to function.

Young people were educated without any religious knowledge. Following the plans dictated from London, they, on the one hand, executed administrative, agricultural, military reorganizations, thus using these activities as show business to distract public attention, and, on the other hand began to devastate Islamic morality, love of ancestors, and national unity. Training agents suitable for their purposes, they located these people in important administrative positions. In those years Europe was taking gigantic strides in physics and chemistry. New discoveries and improvements were being made, and tremendous factories and technical schools were being constructed. All these renovations were being neglected by the Ottomans. On the contrary, subjects such as science, arithmetic, geometry and astronomy, which had been in the curricula of the madrasa system since the reign of Fâtih (Muhammad the Conqueror of Istanbul), were abrogated once and for all. Thus the education of scientifically learned scholars was hampered under the sophistry that "men of religion would not need scientific knowledge." Then, enemies of Islam who came afterwards tried to estrange Muslim children from Islam by saying that "men of religion do not know science. Therefore they are ignorant, backward people." Whatever was harmful to Islam and Muslims would be called 'modern' and 'progressive'. Each law passed would be against the State. Turks, the true owners of the country, would be treated as second class citizens.

Whereas Muslims who would fail to do their military service were fined very high amounts of money which were beyond their ability to pay, the non-Muslims would have to pay very insignificant fines for the same offence. While the real children of this country were being martyred in the wars contrived by the British, the country's industries and trades were gradually being transferred into the hands of non-Muslims and freemasons as a result of the intrigues carried on by Rashîd Pâsha and his masonic henchmen.

Alleging that the Russian Czar Nicholas I was provoking the Orthodox community in Jerusalem against the Catholics, the British urged the Emperor of France Bonaparte III, who was already nervous about any probable Russian power in the Mediterranean, into joining the Crimean War between the Turks and the Russians. This cooperation, which was actually intended for the British interests, was presented to the Turkish people as a result of Rashîd Pâsha's diplomatic accomplishments. It was the Sultân himself, again, who was the first to take notice of these destructive strategies which the enemies were striving to conceal under falsely-adorned advertisements and the ostentation of a counterfeit friendship. He felt such bitter remorse that from time to time he would shut himself up in his private section in the palace and sob bitterly. He would desperately search for ways of fighting against these enemies gnawing at the country and the people, and deploringly beseech Allâhu ta'âlâ for help. Therefore, he dismissed Rashîd Pâsha from the office of Grand Vizier several times, yet each time this foxy man, who had appropriated for himself such nicknames as 'grand' and 'great', somehow managed to overthrow his rivals and resume his position. Unfortunately, the deep feeling of distress and remorse the Sultân had been suffering developed into turberculosis, which in turn put an early end to the young Emperor's life. What remained for Mustafâ Rashîd Pâsha to do in the years to come was to make sure that all sorts of administrative positions, university fellowships and law court presidencies be shared among his disciples only; and he did so, too. Thus he paved the way for a period called the **Qaht-i-rijâl** (scarcity of competent men) in Ottoman history and caused the Ottoman Empire to be called the **Sick Man.**

Ömer Aksu, a professor of economics, says in his article published on the January 22, 1989 issue of the daily **Türkiye** newspaper, "The 1839 Tânzimât Firman has been shown as the starting point of our movement of Westernization. So far we do not appear to have understood the fact that what we should borrow from the West is technology; culture, on the other hand, should remain national. We have looked on Westernization as adoption of Christianity. The trade agreement that Mustafâ Rashîd Pâsha made with the British was the severest blow on our efforts of industrialization."

Scotch masonic lodges carried over their domination in the Ottoman Empire. Pâdishâhs were martyred. Whatever would have been useful for the country and the nation was objected to. Rebellions and revolutions broke out one after another. Who waged the most die-hard struggle against these traitors was Sultân Abd-ul-hamîd Khân II (may his abode be Paradise). They therefore announced him to be the "Red Sultân". Sultân Abd-ul- hamîd improved the Empire economically, opened very many schools and universities, and developed the country. He had a medical faculty built; this school did not have an equal in Europe with the exception of the one in Vienna. A faculty of political sciences was constructed in 1293 [A.D. 1876]. He founded a faculty of law and the Audit Department in 1297. He instituted an engineering department and a boarding high school for girls in 1301. He had water from the Terkos lake conveyed to Istanbul. He had a school for silkworm breeding opened in Bursa, and a school for agriculture and veterinary medicine established at Halkalı. He had a paper factory built at Hamidiyye, a coal-gas factory established at Kadıköy, and a wharf for the Beirut harbour constructed. He had the Ottoman Insurance Company instituted. He had coal mines opened up in Ereğli and Zonguldak. He had an insane asylum established, a hospital called Hamidiyye Etfâl built at Şişli, and the Dâr-ul-aceze instituted. He formed the most powerful army of the world in his time. He had the old and obsolete ships towed into the Golden Horn and reinforced the fleet with high-quality cruisers and battleships newly made in Europe. He had Istanbul-Eskişehir-Ankara, Eskişehir-Adana- Baghdad, and Adana-Damascus-Medina railways built. Thus the world's longest railway network was in the Ottoman country in those days. These works of Abd-ul-hamîd Khân (may his abode be Paradise) have survived to our time. People who travel by train today will see with pride that all the train stations throughout this country are the same ones built during the reign of Abd-ul-hamîd Khân.

Jews, supported and encouraged by the British, were planning to establish a Jewish State in Palestinian territory. Abd-ul-hamîd Khân, who was wise to their Zionistic activities and aspirations and therefore was quite aware of the Jewish threat in the region, advised the Palestinians not to sell the land of Palestine to Jews. Theodor Hertzel, leader of the Universal Zionist Organization, taking Rabbi Moshe Levi with him, visited Sultân Abd-ul-hamîd and requested that Jews be sold land. The Sultân's answer was this: "I would not give you a tiniest piece of land even if all the world's states came to me and poured in front of me all worldly treasures. This land, which cost our ancestors their lives and which has been preserved until today, is not saleable."

Upon this, the Jews cooperated with the party called Union and Progress. All the evil forces on the earth united against the Sultân, eventually dethroning him and orphaning all Muslims, in 1327 [C.E. 1909]. The leaders of the Union and Progress Party filled the highest positions of the State with enemies of the religion and freemasons. In fact, Hayrullah and Mûsâ Kâzım, whom they appointed as Shaikh-ul-islâm respectively, were freemasons. They made the country bloody all over. In the Balkan, Çanakkale (Dardanelles), Russian and Palestinian wars, which were actually caused by British henchmen, the world's biggest armed force founded by Abd-ul-hamîd Khân was annihilated through treacherous and base plans. They martyred hundreds of thousands of innocent youngsters and proved their own perfidious characters by fleeing the country at a time when the country needed unity and protection more than any other time.

Our non-Muslim compatriots who had been seduced in the missionary schools opened in the Ottoman Empire and in churches were provoked to rise against the Ottoman administration. The black-caped spies, who were sent forth under such names as 'teachers for schools' and 'priests for churches', and the so-called newspaper correspondents took money, weapons, and instigation wherever they went. Great rebellions broke out. The massacres perpetrated by Armenians, Bulgarians and Greeks still occupy the pages of history as stains representing human cruelty. It was the British, again, who brought the Greeks to Izmir. Allâhu ta'âlâ showed mercy to the Turkish nation, so that they were able to defend this beautiful country of ours at the end of a great struggle for independence.

When the Ottoman Empire collapsed, the whole world was suffused with a state of utter chaos. The Ottoman Empire had been serving as a buffer between states. It was a protector for Muslims and a deterrent to war between disbelievers. After Sultân Abd-ul-hamîd Khân, there was no more comfort or peace left in any country. Nor did bloodbaths and massacres ever come to an end in Europe, whose states first entered the First World War, then underwent the Second World War, and then were crushed under a Communist invasion and cruelty.

Those nations who had collaborated with the British and attacked the Ottomans from the back were now in such a miserable state that it appeared as if they were never going to enjoy peace again. They were so penitent for their wrongdoing that they began to have the Khutba performed in the name of the Ottoman Khalîfa again. When finally an Israel State was established in Palestine by the British, it became obvious how valuable the Ottoman existence had been. The savageries the Palestinians have been suffering under the Israelite cruelty are being reported in newspapers and shown on television programmes world over. Egyptian Foreign Minister Ahmad Abd- ul-Majîd made the following statement in 1990: "Egypt lived its most comfortable and peaceful days in the time of the Ottomans."

Christian missionaries appear to have been indispensable in places where Europe's Christian countries and America have had interests. These missionaries are hunters of advantages and spoilers of peace hidden behind the simulation of offering service, peace and love to Îsâ (Jesus) 'alaihis-salâm', whom they divinize, (may Allâhu ta'âlâ protect us against such heresy). Their more important task is to make the countries they have been assigned dependent on Christian countries. Missionaries learn perfectly the languages, customs and traditions of the countries they are going to go to. As soon as they begin their mission in a country, they study its political status, military power, geographical position, economic level, and religious structure to the tiniest details, and report their findings to the Christian government they are working for. Wherever they go they find people to collaborate with and hire these people. While still bearing names identical with those of the native people, these people are now either Christianized ignoramuses or hired traitors.

A candidate missionary is trained either in the country where he is to carry on his mission or by another missionary trained in that country.

Missionary activities increased in the aftermath of the **Gülhâne Firmân** prepared and proclaimed by Rashîd Pâsha, the freemason. Colleges were opened in the most beautiful places of Anatolia. **Fırat** (Euphrates) **College** was opened in Harput in 1276 [A.D. 1859]. No degree of expense was deemed too much in building this school. In the meantime missionaries established sixty-two centres on the plain of Harput, and twenty-one churches were built. Missionary organisations were instituted in sixty-two of the sixty- six Armenian villages and one church was constructed for every three villages. All the Armenians, regardless of what age, were antagonized against the Ottomans, and female missionaries spared no effort to train Armenian women and girls for this purpose. The notorious woman missionary Maria A. West wrote the following explanation in her book 'Romance of Mission', which she published afterwards: "We penetrated the souls of the Armenians. We carried out a revolution in their lives." This activity was conducted in any place with an Armenian population. Antep College in Gâziantep, Anadolu College in Merzifon, and Robert College in Istanbul are only a few examples. The Merzifon College, for instance, did not have any Turkish students. Of its one hundred and thirty-five students, one hundred and eight were Armenians and twenty-seven were Byzantines. These students were boarders collected from all parts of Anatolia. The director was a priest, like in the others. In the meantime a kind of boiling motion began in Anatolia. Militants from the clandestine Armenian Society ruthlessly killed Muslims and burned Muslim villages, recognizing no right to live for the Ottomans, who were the guards, the owners of the country. The Armenians were pursued and an operation of retaliation and repression was executed in 1311 [C.E. 1893], whereupon it was found out that the militants were camouflaged in that college and planned all their activities there, and that their chieftains were two college teachers named Kayayan and Tumayan. Upon this the missionaries raised a universal clamour. In order to save the two villainous Armenians, great public demonstrations were arranged in America and England. Strange to say, this event was a cause of discord between Britain and the Ottoman Empire. And what is even more strange is that when the demonstrations arranged by the British missionaries were held in 1893, the Director of the Merzifon Anadolu College was in London, and among the demonstrators, too. The massacre of Muslims in Anatolia, which were perpetrated by Christians, were later reflected in the books of Christian writers in totally the opposite way. One of these lies is written in Mer'ash chapter of Arabic dictionary **Al-Munjid,** a book prepared in Beirut.

In 1893, three million copies of the Bible and four million other Christian books were distributed by missionaries to the Armenians in Turkey. Accordingly, every one of the Armenians, including the newly born babies, was given seven books. The amount of money spent yearly by the American missionaries alone was 285,000 dollars. To elucidate how great an amount this money was, we would like to state that seventeen hundred and twenty-eight gigantic schools like the Merzifon Anadolu College could have been constructed by an equal expenditure.

It would be sheer credulity to think that it was

religious zeal that motivated the missionaries to dispense with this stupendous sum of money. For religion is a trade in the eyes of missionaries. This amount of money, which the missionaries spent in Anatolia for the purpose of demolishing Islam and extirpating the Ottoman nation, was a tiny fraction of the money they had collected through propagations that "Turks are massacring Armenians. Let us help them."

It was around the same years when our Greek compatriots in Athens and Yenişehir, incited by the missionaries in colleges and churches and supported by tremendous armed forces from Britain, revolted and wildly massacred hundreds of thousands of Muslims, children and women alike. This rebellion was quelled by forces under Edhem Pâsha's command in 1313 [A.D. 1895]. This was a victory which was achieved not only against the Greek forces, but also against the British, the real inciters.

Britain is governed by three authorities: The King, Parliament, and the Church (i.e. Westminister). Up until the year 918 [A.D. 1512], the parliament and the king's palace was within Westminister. After the conflagration in 1512, the king moved to Buckingham Palace, and parliament and the church remained under the same roof. In Britain the church and the state are interlaced. Kings and Queens are crowned by the archbishop in church.

According to a report entitled "Social Inclinations" and published by the British Central Bureau of Statistics, out of every hundred babies born in Britain, twenty-three are born as a result of illegitimate relations.

According to a statistical report announced by the British metropolitan police Scotland Yard and published in an Istanbul daily newspaper dated May 7, 1990, there is no more security of life in London, which has become a very dangerous city, particularly for women. According to the British police reports, in the last twelve years there has been an increase in all sorts of offences, mainly rapes and robberies.

Family, in all countries and religions, is an institution formed by a man and a woman who have come together in a legitimate way. On the other hand, British laws have legitimized and protected two men's practising homosexual acts.

It is stated in a report headed 'Scandal in the British army' which appeared in a daily Istanbul newspaper dated November 12, 1987, that the newly enlisted lance corporals in the Guards regiment belonging to Queen Elizabeth II were sexually harassed and were subjected to sadistic torture.

In a research article published in the December 28, 1990, issue of the daily **Türkiye,** it is reported that the rate of homosexuals in British churches has reached 15 per cent and their number in the Houses of Lords and Commons is even higher. Indecencies have spread out to the Parliament and scandals like Profumo have erupted. Britain is the first European country where homosexuals formed an organization. Even in places where such indecencies are practised, British hostility against Islam is quite conspicuous. The back streets of London, where adultery, pederasty and all the other sorts of indecencies are committed, are painted green, a colour Islam holds sacred, and tablets depicting Mekka hang on the doors of these dens of abhorrence.

According to a report published in the British daily newspaper **Guardian,** two hundred thousand girls resorted to law courts and asked for protection against their fathers who had been harassing them sexually since they had reached the age of puberty. According to the BBC, on the other hand, the number of those who did not resort to law courts (though having been subjected to the same abominable treatment) is estimated to be around five million.

With respect to land shares, Britain has the most inequitable system world over. The ceaseless struggles waged by British peasants against lords are recorded in history. It is a fact that even today eighty per cent of British land is possessed by a privileged minority.

It is written in the May 31, 1992 Sunday edition of **Türkiye**, "Unemployment and poverty which was caused by economic depression increases the suicides in England. It was reported in the British Medical periodical that a study which was carried out by two doctors from Oxford Hospital showed that every year a hundred thousand people commit suicide and 4500 of them died. Of them, 62 percent were young girls." No other State as treacherous, aggressive and wild as the British who martyred hundreds of thousands of Muslims every year and who led hundreds of thousands of their own people to commit suicide has been witnessed.

Ireland, on the other hand, has become a nuisance to

Britain. We hope that we shall all live up to see those happy days when they will fall into the traps they have set for us.

In order to bless ourselves with the blessed name of Sayyid Abd-ul-hakîm Arwâsî 'rahmatullâhi aleyh', we would like to end the second section of our book with his following statements, which define the British in a way covering all the main points while leaving out any points that are not relevant:

"The British are the greatest enemies of Islam. Let us compare Islam to a tree; other disbelievers will fell this tree by cutting it by the lowest point of its trunk whenever they have the opportunity. Consequently, Muslims will begin feeling hostility towards them. Yet this tree may send forth roots some day. British policy, on the other hand, is quite different. He will serve this tree; he will feed it. So Muslims will develop a liking for him. However, one night, when all the people are sound asleep, he will administer poison to its root without anyone noticing it. The tree will dry up for good and will never sprout again. He will go on duping Muslims by expressing his solidarity with them. This exemplification of poisoning represents the British stratagem of extirpating Islamic scholars, Islamic literature and Islamic learning through the hypocritical and ignoble natives he has hired in return for the appeasement of sensuous desires, such as money, rank, positions and women."

May Allâhu ta'âlâ protect all Muslims against all sorts of evil. May He protect statesmen, Islamic scholars and all Muslims from falling for the deceit and tricks of missionaries and the British and from serving them!

Hüseyin Hilmi Işık

Part III

Yûsuf Nebhânî

KHULÂSA-T-UL-KELÂM

The following chapter is the translation of the booklet Khulâsa-t-ul-kelâm:

This booklet is in Arabic. Its author, Yûsuf Nebhânî, passed away in Beirut in 1305 H. [1932 A.D.] May hamd (praise, laud and thanks) be to Allâhu ta'âlâ! He blesses anyone He likes with hidâyat (guidance to the right way and consequently to salvation) and leaves anyone He wishes in dalâlat (aberration, wrong way). [With His justice He accepts the prayers of those who wish to be saved from dalâlat and attain eternal felicity.] We pronounce benedictions over our master, Muhammad 'alaihis-salâm', who is the highest of Prophets and of all the selected people. May blessings and salutations be upon his Âl (close relatives, household) and upon all his As-hâb, who shine on the earth like stars in the sky!

This small booklet has few pages. Yet it is rich with respect to the knowledge it contains. People of knowledge and wisdom will accept it if they read it with common sense, and those who are blessed with the hidâyat of Allâhu ta'âlâ, with the right way, will believe it outright. This booklet distinguishes the **Sirât-i-mustaqîm,** which is a blessing Allâhu ta'âlâ has bestowed on Muslims, from the way of **Dalâlat,** wherein He has forsaken His enemies. I have named this booklet **Khulâsa-t-ul-kelâm fî terjîh-i-dîn-il-Islâm,** which means 'a summary of the statements which will help choose the Islamic religion.'

163

O man, who wishes to save himself from eternal torment and to attain infinite blessings! If you spent all your time pondering over this very important, very great truth, if you applied all your energies to find out the means for safeguarding yourself against endless torment, when you were alone and in all situtations, if you cooperated with all other people and struggled to the best of your abilities as a human being to attain this goal, all these endeavors would be extremely insignificant when compared with the importance of this means. In fact, it would be similar to giving a grain of sand in return for all worldly treasures. The importance of this truth could not be explained through this writing of ours. This writing of ours is intended to give some clues to the wise. A single implication will suffice for a wise person to realise the purport. I, therefore, shall make a few clue-bearing statements to prime the pump for this realisation: Man forms a liking to his settled tendencies. He does not want to cease from doing them. When he is born, for instance, be gets used to sucking milk, and hates to get weaned. As he grows, he becomes accustomed to his home, to his quarter, to his hometown. It becomes very difficult for him to part with them. Later on, he becomes wont to his shop, to his profession, to his scientific branch, to his family, to his language and religion, and hates to part with them. Thus various communities, tribes, nations come into being. Then, a nation's love of their religion is not the result of a realization that their religion is the best of religions. A wise person should study his religion, compare it with other religions, find out what religion is the true one and hold fast to it. For adherence to a wrong religion will drift one to eternal disasters and everlasting torments. O man, wake up from oblivion! If you say, "How do I know what religion is the true one? I believe that the religion I am accustomed to is the true one. I love this religion," then you should know that "Religion means to obey the commandments and prohibitions which Allah has sent through Prophets." These injunctions are men's duties to their Rabb (Allah) and to one another.

Of all the existing religions, which one gives the most helpful explanation of the Rabb's Attributes, of worships, and of the relations between creatures? Wisdom is a sense which distinguishes between good and bad. What is bad should be rejected and what is good should be studied. Studying a religion means studying its beginning, its Prophet, his As-hâb (companions) and Ummat (followers), especially the notable ones. If you like them, choose that religion! Follow your mind, not your nafs! Your nafs will mislead you by infusing feelings of shame and fear into you pertaining to your family, your friends and wicked and miscreant men of religion. The harms such people may give you is a mere nothing when compared with everlasting torment. A person who realizes this fact fully will choose the **Dîn- i-islâm.** He will believe in Muhammad 'alaihis-salâm', who is the last Prophet. Besides, Islam enjoins a belief in all Prophets. It teaches that their religions and canonical laws were true, that each new Messenger invalidated the Sharî'ats prior to him, and that by the same token the advent of Muhammad's 'alaihis-salâm' Sharî'at invalidated all the earlier Sharî'ats. A person's realizing that the religion he has been used to following is a wrong one, abandoning this religion and having îmân in Muhammad 'alaihis-salâm' will be very difficult for his nafs to tolerate. For the nafs has been created in a nature inimical to Allâhu ta'âlâ, to Muhammad 'alaihis-salâm', and to his Sharî'at. This inimical nature of the nafs is called **Hamîyat-ul-jâhiliyya** (mistaken zeal, fanaticism, bigotry). Parents, teachers, vicious friends, [radio and television programs, statesmen] in the wrong religion will support this bigoted feeling. Hence the saying, "Teaching the child is like inscribing on stone." For eliminating this bigotry it is necessary to strive hard, to struggle against the nafs, and to convince the nafs through reason. If you read my following writings with attention, it will help you with this struggle of yours:

Adapting oneself to a certain religion is for attaining eternal happiness and securing oneself against everlasting disasters. It is not for boasting about a religion which one has inherited from one's parents. And each Prophet is a human being who possesses the qualifications of prophethood and conveys the injunctions of Allâhu ta'âlâ to His born slaves. One has to adapt oneself to a Prophet who has these qualifications and enter his religion. People who worship icons and idols called Wasanî (Vesenî) and godless people called Dehrî, [also freemasons and communists] are like beasts. Also, the Nazarene (Christian) and Judaic religions have become obsolete for the following reasons:

1- In the Islamic religion, Allâhu ta'âlâ has attributes of perfection. He does not have attributes of deficiency. The worships are easy to perform. Social relations are based on justice. Worships and social relations taught in the other religions, however, have changed in the course of time, so that they are no

---

longer reasonable or practicable.

2- A comparative study of the lives of Muhammad, Îsâ (Jesus) and Mûsâ (Moses) 'alaihimus-salâm' will show that Muhammad 'alaihis-salâm' is of the highest lineage, the noblest, the bravest, the most beneficent, the most knowledgeable, the wisest, the most superior, and the most sagacious in knowledge pertaining to this world and the next. On the other hand, he was ummî (illiterate). In other words, he had never read books nor learned anything from anybody.

3- The mu'jizas (miracles) worked through Muhammad 'alaihis-salâm' were much more numerous than the total of those wrought through the others. The mu'jizas of the others are past and over. A number of Muhammad's 'alaihis-salâm' mu'jizas, on the other hand, especially the mu'jiza of Qur'ân al-kerîm, have been continuing and will last till the end of the world. And the kerâmats[80] of his Ummat (Muslims), especially those wrought through the Awliyâ,[81] have been occurring continually and everywhere.

4- Among the reports communicating these three religions to us, those which are conveyed through Qur'ân al-kerîm and Hadîth-i-sherîfs are more numerous and more dependable. All of them have been

---

[80] An extraordinary event which Allâhu ta'âlâ creates through a person whom He loves is called a wonder, or a miracle. When a miracle occurs through a Prophet it is termed a mu'jiza. When it occurs through a Walî, i.e. a person loved by Allâhu ta'âlâ, it is called a kerâmet. Please see our book Proof of Prophethood.

[81] Plural form of Walî.

committed to books and spread throughout the world. Muhammad 'alaihis-salâm' was forty years old when he was informed that he was the Prophet. And he was sixty-three years old when he passed away. His prophethood lasted for twenty-three years. He passed away after the entire Arabic peninsula had obeyed him, after his religion had spread and had been learned everywhere, after his call had been heard in the east and in the west, and after the number of his As-hâb had reached 150 thousand. He performed his Farewell Hajj together with his 120 thousand Sahâbîs, and passed away eighty days after this. The third âyat-i-kerîma of Mâida sûra, which purports, **"Today I have completed your religion and consummated my blessing on you and called Islam as your religion,"** was revealed during this Hajj. All these Sahâbîs were faithful and true. Most of them were profoundly learned in Islam and were Awliyâ. They spread Rasûlullah's religion and mu'jizas over the earth. For they travelled to other countries for Jihâd. Whereever they went they conveyed the religious teachings and mu'jizas to men of knowledge living there. And these people, in their turn, taught others. Thus, scholars living in each century taught many other scholars belonging to the next generations. And these scholars wrote these teachings in thousands of books, and also wrote the names of those people who conveyed these teachings. They classified the hadîth-i-sherîfs they learned in a number of categories and gave them such terms as Sahîh, Hasan, etc. They did not let false statements fabricated by liars [and Jews] in the name of hadîths enter their books. They were very stringent, extremely sensitive in this respect. Owing to their stringent efforts the Islamic religion was established on very solid foundations and spread without any change. None of the other religions spread in such a healthy way. The mu'jizas of our beloved Prophet Muhammad 'alaihissalâm', substantially proves that he is the true Prophet. Islam's fundamental and essential teachings, existence and unity of Allâhu ta'âlâ, His Attributes of perfection, prophethood of Muhammad 'alaihis-salâm', that he was faithful and dependable and the highest of all Prophets, that people will rise again after death and will be called to account, the bridge of Sirât, blessings of Paradise, torments in Hell, that it is farz (a plain Islamic commandment) to perform the prayer called namâz five times daily, the farz (obligatory) parts of early and late afternoon and night prayers have four rak'ats each, that (the farz part of) morning prayer contains two rak'ats and (that of) evening prayer contains three rak'ats, that it is farz to begin fasting when the new moon for the month of Ramadân is seen in the sky and to celebrate the Bayram (feast) called Fitr when the new moon for the month of Shawwâl is seen, that it is farz (or fard) to perform (the worship called) Hajj once in one's lifetime, that it is harâm (forbidden) [for women and girls to go out without covering their heads, their hair, (for everyone, men and women alike) to practise pederasty] to commit fornication, to drink wine [or even a drop of any hard drink which would intoxicate in case it were taken in large amounts], for a person who is junub (canonically unclean, needing a ritual washing) and for a menstruating woman to perform namâz, to perform namâz without a ritual ablution, and all the other essential religious teachings were conveyed correctly to all Muslims, educated and ignorant ones alike, and eventually to us without any changes having been made in them. This fact is known by reasonable Christians and Jews as well. These people acknowledge that the means by which they learned their own religion do not have equally dependable authenticity. Because Muhammad's 'alaihis-salâm' time is closer to ours and because the number of scholars who conveyed the Islamic religion to us is enormous, it has not been possible to insert superstitions into Islam. Christianity and Judaism do not possess these two blessings. There is a space of about six hundred years [according to historians] between the bi'that [appearing] of Îsâ 'alaihis-salâm' and that of Muhammad 'alaihis-salâm'. For [they say] that there are six hundred and twenty-one years between Îsâ's 'alaihis- salâm' birth and Muhammad's 'alaihis-salâm' hijra (migration) from Mekka to Medîna. [On the other hand, this space of time is one thousand years according to Islamic scholars.] During this space of time ignorance was widespread all over the earth. It was therefore very difficult to distinguish between true reports and false ones.

Îsâ's 'alaihis-salâm' call did not last long. Allâhu ta'âlâ raised him up to heaven when he was thirty-three years old. During this short time he was weak and defenceless against unbelievers. The conditions were not convenient enough for him to carry out successfully the duty which his Rabb had assigned to him. The time's Jewish community and their government were an additional impediment. Nor did he have any supporters except those few people called Hawârîs (Apostles). His only believers were these twelve Apostles, who were no more than poor, ignorant hunters. After his ascension[82]

---

[82] Contrary to the Christian credo, which theorizes that Îsâ 'alaihis- salâm'

to heaven, various reports and narrations were compiled in [four] books called the Injîl, which, being transferred from one incompetent hand to another and being translated from one language to another, underwent various interpolations. Much of the information contained in these gospels therefore is contradictory with one another and illogical. In fact, reports given in one of them confute and belie those written in another. The same case applies to different versions of the same gospel. To eliminate these differences and contradictions, priests had to convene in every century and correct the existing gospels, thus making additions and excisions and meanwhile inserting absurdities that have nothing to do with religion. They forced people to believe these books. Most of the statements in these books do not belong to Îsâ 'alaihis-salâm' or to his Apostles. As a result, they parted into various groups. New sects appeared in every century. Most of them dissented from earlier ones. And they all know that the gospels they have now are not the holy book teaching the religion revealed to Îsâ 'alaihis-salâm'.

So are the Judaic books narrating the religion and the mu'jizas of Mûsâ 'alaihis-salâm'. The space of time here is longer. Mûsâ 'alaihis-salâm' passed away two thousand three hundred and forty-eight (2348) years before Muhammad's 'alaihis-salâm' hijrat. During the long time of ignorance between them it was impossible to convey the Judaic religion correctly. In addition,

---

was crucified and then ascended to heaven, Islam teaches that this exalted Prophet was not crucified, and that Allâhu ta'âlâ raised him, alive, up to heaven. Please see our book *Could Not Answer*.

Jewish men of religion were killed by cruel tyrants like Nebuchadnezzar, and others were taken as captives and transported from the Bayt-ul-muqaddas to Babylon. In fact, there were times when Jerusalem did not contain one single person educated well enough to read the Torah. Danyâl (Daniel) 'alaihis- salâm' knew the Torah by heart, so that he would recite and dictate it. This served to delay its being interpolated only till after this blessed Prophet's death. As a matter of fact, the additions made after him were far too amoral to be attributed to Allâhu ta'âlâ or to Prophets.

That ignorance did not become widespread after the time of Muhammad 'alaihis-salâm' is known by all peoples. In fact, knowledge became a widespread common attribute among all Muslims, great Islamic states were established and they spread knowledge, science, justice and human rights everywhere. Now, if a wise and reasonable person examines these three religions, he will definitely adapt himself to Islam. For the purpose is to find the true religion. Lying and slandering are harâm in Islam. Âyat-i- kerîmas and hadîth-i-sherîfs vehemently prohibit these two vices. When it is a grave sin to slander an ordinary person, it is much worse, much more harâm to slander the Messenger of Allah. For this reason, there cannot be any lies, any errors in books telling about Muhammad 'alaihis-salâm' and his mu'jizas. A wise person should overcome his pertinacity, abandon the religion that will lead to perdition, and adapt himself to the true religion which will guide him to happiness. Life in this world is very short. Its days are passing by and turning into mere visions one by one. Every human being will end in death, whereafter there is either eternal torment or an everlasting life of blessings. And their time is approaching everybody with great speed.

O man! Have mercy on yourself! Remove the curtain of oblivion from your mind! See what is wrong as wrong and try to get rid of it! See what is right as right and adapt yourself to it, hold fast to it! The decision you will make is very great, very important. And the time is very short. You will certainly die! Think of the time when you will die! Prepare yourself for what you are going to experience! You will not escape everlasting torment unless you adapt yourself to Haqq. Repenting when it is too late will be useless. Confirming the truth at the last breath will not be accepted. Making tawba after death will not be valid. That day, if Allâhu ta'âlâ says, "O My slave! I gave thee the light of mind. I commanded thee to use it for knowing Me and for having belief in Me, in My Prophet Muhammad 'alaihis-salâm', and in the Islamic religion revealed through him. I informed in the Torah and the Bible about the advent of this Prophet. I spread his name and religion in every country. You cannot say you did not hear about him. You worked day and night for worldly earnings, worldly pleasures. You never thought of what you were going to experience in the Hereafter. In a state of unawareness you fell into the talons of death," how will you answer?

O man! Think of what is going to happen to you! Come to your senses before your lifetime is over. People you had been seeing around you, you had been talking to, you had been sympathizing with, you had been afraid of, died one by one. They do not exist now. They came and went by like fancies. Think well! What a horrible thought it is to burn in eternal fire! And how great a fortune it is to live in everlasting blessings. You have the choice now. Everybody will end up in one of these two extremes. Another alternative is impossible. It would be utter ignorance, insanity not to consider this and take precautions accordingly. May Allâhu ta'âlâ bless us all with following reason! Âmîn.

It is stated as follows in the book **Qawl-us-sabt fî rad-d-i-'alâ deâw-il-protestanet:** Allâma Rahmatullah Hindî[83] states in his book **(Iz-hâr-ul-haqq),** "Before the beginning of Islam there were no original copies of the Torah or the Bible left anywhere. The existing ones today are history books made up of true and false reports. The Torah and the Bible mentioned in Qur'ân al-kerîm are not the existing books in the name of Torah and Bible. Of the teachings written in these books, the ones affirmed by Qur'ân al- kerîm are true and those which it rejects are false. We would not say true or false about those which are not mentioned in Qur'ân al-kerîm. There is no documentary evidence to prove that the four Gospels are the word of Allah. A British priest with whom I spoke with in India admitted this fact and said that all the documents in this respect had been lost through tumults that had happened in the world until A.D. 313". It is written in the second volume of the interpretation of the Bible by Heron, in the sixty- fifth page of the first volume of the historian Moshem's history, printed in 1332 [A.D. 1913], and in the hundred and twenty-fourth page of the fifth volume of the explanation of the Bible by Lardis that the Gospels underwent various interpolations. Jerome says,

---

[83] Rahmatullah Hindî passed away in Mekka in 1306 [A.D. 1889]

"As I translated the Bible, I saw that different copies contradicted one another." Adam Clark says in the first volume of his interpretation, "The Bible underwent various interpolations during its translation into Latin. Contradictory additions were made." Ward Catholic says on the eighteenth page of his interpretation, printed in 1841, "Oriental heretics changed many parts of the Bible. Protestant priests submitted a report to King James I and said: The Psalms in our book of prayers are unlike the ones that are in Hebrew. There are almost two hundred changes. On the other hand, Protestant priests made even more changes." Numerous examples of these changes are given in the book **Iz-hâr- ul-haqq.** Interpolations in various editions of the Gospels are exemplified also in the book **Al-fâsilu-bayn-al-haqq wa'l-bâtil,** by Izz-ad-dîn Muhammadî, and **Tuhfat-ul-erîb,** by Abdullah Terjumân.

All priests know that Îsâ 'alaihis-salâm' did not write anything. Neither did he leave behind any written documents nor have anyone write anything. He did not teach his Sharî'at in written form. After his ascension to heaven, disagreements began among the Nazarenes. They could not come together to consolidate their religious knowledge. As a result, more than fifty Gospels were written. Four of them were chosen. Eight years after Îsâ 'alaihis- salâm' the Gospel of **Matthew** was written in the Syrian language in Palestine. The orignial copy of this Gospel does not exist today. There is a book said to be its Greek version. The Gospel of **Mark** was written in Rome thirty years after him. The Gospel of **Luke** was written in Greek in Alexandria twenty-eight years after him. And thirty-eight years after him, the Gospel of **John** was written in Ephesus. All these Gospels contain narrations, stories, and events that happened after Îsâ 'alaihis-salâm'. Luke and Mark are not among the Apostles. They wrote what they had heard from others. Authors of these Gospels did not call their books Injîl (Bible). They said that theirs were history books. Those who called them the Bible were those who translated them afterwards.

This book, **Qawl-us-sebt,** was written in 1341 [A.D. 1923] by Sayyid Abd-ul-qâdir Iskenderânî as a response to the book **Aqâwîl-ul-Qur'âniyya,** written in Arabic and printed by a Protestant priest in Egypt; in 1990, (Hakîkat Kitâbevî) reproduced this book together with the books **As-sirât-ul-musteqîm** and **Khulâsa-t-ul-kelâm.**

The original Injîl was in the Hebrew language and was destroyed by the Jews when they arrested Îsâ 'alaihis-salâm' for the purpose of crucifying him. Not even a single copy of the original Holy Book was written during the three years, the period of Îsâ's 'alaihis-salâm' call. Christians deny the original Injîl. The four Gospels which they call the Bible do not contain any system of worship. All they contain are the discussions between Îsâ 'alaihis-salâm' and the Jews. However, a religious book must teach forms of worship. If they should claim to have been doing their worship in accordance with the Torah, then why do they ignore its very important commandments such as observing the Sabbath [on Saturday], circumcision, and abstention from eating pork? Their Gospels do not contain any information telling that these commandments should be disregarded. On the other hand, Qur'ân al-kerîm covers detailed knowledge pertaining to all sorts of worships, ethics, law, trade, agriculture, and science, and encourages these branches. It prescribes solutions for all sorts of physical and spiritual problems.

For fourteen hundred years no poet, no man of literature, no obdurate unbeliever has been able to express a statement similar to any one âyat of Qur'ân al-kerîm, try as they would. That not a single one of its âyats could be said in its exactitude, despite the fact that the vocabulary used in it consists of commonly used ordinary words, shows clearly that it is a mu'jiza (miracle wrought through a Prophet). The other mu'jizas of Muhammad 'alaihis- salâm' are past events; they exist only in name today. As for Qur'ân al-kerîm; it shines as brightly as the sun, always and everywhere. It is a medicine for every illness, a remedy for every disease. Allâhu ta'âlâ, the Most Kind, has bestowed it on His Habîb-i-akram (Blessed beloved one) and revealed it to him so that all His slaves would be happy. With His infinite Kindness and Compassion, He has protected it against changes and interpolations. He did not make this promise concerning other heavenly books.

The sharî'ats of all Prophets, having been suited (by Allâhu ta'âlâ) to the requirements of the times they lived in, were naturally different from one another. Tenets of belief, however, were identical in all of them. They all taught that Allâhu ta'âlâ is One, and that there will be a resurrection after death. It is stated in the thirty-ninth verse of the Deuteronomy: "... the LORD he is God in heaven above, and upon the earth beneath: there is none else." (Deut: 4-19), and in the sixth chapter: "Hear, O Israel: The LORD our God is one LORD:" (Ibid: 6-4). In II Chronicles Suleymân (Solomon) 'alaihis-salâm' is quoted as having said, "... O LORD God of Israel, there is no God like thee in the heaven, nor in the earth; ..." (2 Chr: 6-14) "... behold, heaven and the heaven of heavens cannot contain thee; how much less this house which I have built!" (Ibid: 6-18) after building the Bayt-ul- muqqaddas (the Masjîd al-Aqsâ in Jerusalem). It is written in the fifteenth chapter of I Samuel that Prophet **Samuel** said, "... the Strength of Israel will not lie nor repent: for he is not a man, that he should repent." (Sam: 15-29) It is stated as follows in the forty- fifth chapter of the book attributed to Prophet **Isaiah:** "I am the LORD, and there is none else, ..." (Is: 45-5) "I form the light, and create darkness: I make peace, and create evil: ..." (Ibid: 45-7) It is written in the nineteenth chapter of the Gospel of Matthew, "And, behold, one came and said unto him, Good Master, what good thing shall I do, that I may have eternal life?" "And he said unto him, Why callest thou me good? there is none good but one, that is, God: but if thou wilt enter into life, keep the commandments." (Matt: 19-16, 17) It is stated as follows in the twelfth chapter of Mark: "And one of the scribes came, and ... asked him, Which is the first commandment of all?" "And Jesus answered him, The first of all the commandments is, Hear, O Israel; The Lord our God is one Lord:" "And thou shalt love the Lord thy God with all thy heart, and with all thy soul, and with all thy mind, and with all thy strength: ..." (Mark: 12-28, 29, 30) Muhammad 'alaihis-salâm' stated so, too.

A person who contradicts [disbelieves] Muhammad 'alaihis- salâm' will have disbelieved all the Prophets. Belief in **Trinity** [existence of three Gods] means to deny all the Prophets. The doctrine of the Trinty appeared long after Îsâ's 'alaihis-salâm' ascension to heaven. Formerly, all the **Nazarites** held the belief of **Tawhîd** (Unity of Allah) and observed most of the principles in the Torah. When a number of idolaters and Greek philosophers joined the Nazarites they mixed their former belief, the Trinity, with the Nazarene religion. It is written in a French book, which was translated into Arabic and given the title **Qurrat-un-nufûs,** that the person who interpolated the doctrine of the Trinity into the Nazarene religion first was a priest named Seblius, in the year 200 of the Christian Era, and that this first interpolation caused much bloodshed. At that time many scholars defended the belief of Unity and said that Îsâ 'alaihis-salâm' was a human being and a Prophet. It was sometime around the year 300 when Arius of Alexandria proclaimed the belief of Unity and announced that the doctrine of the Trinity was wrong and void. In the (first) Nicene council convened by Constantine the Great in 325, belief in the Unity was rejected and Arius was excommunicated. They themselves do not know what they mean by the name **Holy Ghost** (or Spirit), which they suppose to be the third god of the Trinity. They say that it was the Holy Ghost through which Îsâ 'alaihis- salâm' came into being in the womb of his mother, Mary. Islam teaches that the Rûh-ul-Quds (the Holy Spirit) is the Archangel named Jebrâîl (Gabriel).[84]

---

[84] The Turkish book Izâh-ul-merâm was written by Abdullah Abdî bin Destân Mustafâ Bey of Manastir 'rahmatullâhi aleyh'. He passed away in

Shams-ad-dîn Sâmî Bey wrote in the 1316 [A.D. 1898] edition of **Kâmûs-ul-a'lâm:** The Islamic Prophet is Muhammad 'alaihis- salâm'. His father is Abdullah and his grandfather is Abd-ul- muttalib bin Hishâm bin 'Abd-i-Menâf bin Qusey bin Kilâb. According to historians, he was born in Mekka towards a Monday morning, which coincided with the twelfth day of Rabî'ul-awwal month, the twentieth of April, in 571 A.D. His mother is Âmina, the daughter of Wahab, and his grandfather is 'Abd-i-Menaf bin Zuhra bin Kilâb. Kilâb is Abdullah's great grandfather. Abdullah passed away at a place called **Dâr-un-nâbigha** in the vicinity of Medîna on his way back from a commercial expedition to Damascus. He was twenty-five years old. He did not see his son. He (Muhammad 'alaihis-salâm') stayed with his wet nurse Halîma among her tribe for five years. This tribe, which was called Benî Sa'îd, were the most eloquent people of Arabia. For this reason, Muhammad 'alaihis-salâm' spoke very eloquently. When he was six years old Âmina, (his blessed mother), took him to his maternal uncles in Medîna and passed away there. His nurse, Umm-i-Eymen, took him to Mekka and delivered him to Abd-ul- muttalib, (his blessed paternal grandfather). He was eight years old, when Abd-ul-muttalib passed away and he began to stay in the home of his paternal uncle Abû Tâlib. When he was twelve years old he joined Abû Tâlib on a commercial journey to Damascus. When he was seventeen years old his paternal uncle Zubeyr took him to Yemen. When he was twenty-five years old he went to Damascus as the

---

1303 [A.D. 1885]. The book was printed in the printhouse that belonged to Yahyâ Efendi, the shaikh of Mustafâ Pâsha convent immediately outside Edirnekapı, Istanbul.

leader of Hadîja's 'radiy-Allâhu anhâ' caravan on a commercial expedition. He became famous for his excellent manners, beautiful moral character, and industrious habits. Two months later he married Hadîja. When he was forty years old the angel named Jebrâ'îl (Gabriel) visited him and he was informed of his prophethood. Hadîja was his first Believer, and she was followed by Abû Bekr, then Alî, who was a child yet, and then Zeyd bin Hârisa. When he was forty-three years old he was ordered to invite everybody to Islam. Heathens persecuted him severely. He was fifty-three years old when he migrated to Medîna-i-munawwara. He arrived in the Kubâ village of Medîna on Monday the eighth of Rabî'ul-awwal, which coincided with the twentieth day of September, in the 622nd year of the Christian era. It was during the cliphate of hadrat 'Umar when this year, (i.e. A.D. 622), was accepted as the beginning of the Muslim era and the first day of the month of Muharram as the first day (new year's day) of the **Hijrî Lunar** year. It was the sixteenth day, a Friday, in the month of July. And the twentieth day of September was accepted as the first day of the Hijrî Solar year. The 623rd new year's day of the Christian era took place during the first hijrî solar and lunar years. When the first commandment to perform Ghazâ and Jihâd against the unbelievers was given (by Allâhu ta'âlâ), the **Ghazâ** (Holy War) of **Bedr** was made in the second year of the Hijrat. Of the nine-hundred-and-fifty-strong army of unbelievers, fifty were killed and forty-four were taken as captives. In the third year, the **Ghazâ** of **Uhud** was made. The number of unbelievers was three thousand, whereas Muslims numbered seven hundred. Seventy-five Sahâbîs were martyred. In the fourth year the **Ghazâ** of **Hendek** (Trench) and in the fifth year the **Ghazâ** of **Benî Mustalaq** were made. It was during this same year when women were commanded to cover themselves. The **Ghazâ** of **Hayber** and the peace agreement called **Bî'at-ur-ridwân,** at Hudaybiya, were made in the sixth year. In the seventh year the Kaiser and the Chosroes were sent letters of invitation to Islam. In the eighth year the **Ghazâ** of **Mûta** was conducted against the Byzantine army under Heraclius' command, Mekka was conquered and the **Ghazâ** of **Huneyn** was accomplished. In the ninth year an expedition for the **Ghazâ** of **Tabuk** was made. In the tenth year the **Hajj** of **Wedâ'** (Farewell) was made. In the eleventh year, after suffering fever for thirteen days, the blessed Prophet passed away in the room adjacent to his masjîd on Monday the twelfth of Rabî'ul awwal, when he was sixty-three years old.

Rasûlullah 'sall-Allâhu alaihi wa sallam' was always affable and softspoken. There was a nûr shining on his blessed face. Those who saw him would fall in love with him. His mildness, patience, beautiful moral habits are written in thousands of books. He had four sons and four daughters from Hadîja 'radiy-Allâhu anhâ'. And he had one son from Mâriya of Egypt. All his children except Fâtima passed away while he was alive. This is the end of our citation from **Kâmûs-ul-a'lâm.**

Imâm-i-Ghazâlî wrote in his book **Kimyâ-i Sa'âdat,** "Allâhu ta'âlâ sent Prophets to His slaves. Through these great people He informed His slaves about ways guiding to happiness and those leading to disasters. The highest, the most superior and the last of the Prophets is **Muhammad** 'alaihis-salâm'. He is the Prophet for all people, for all nations. All people all over the world have to believe in that exalted Prophet." A person who believes in him and adapts himself to him will attain blessings in the world and in the Hereafter. He who does not believe in him, on the other hand, will be subjected to everlasting torment in the Hereafter.

Yûsuf Nebhânî

CONCLUSION

In short, **Din** (religion) means the system of rules revealed by Allâhu ta'âlâ to Prophets in order to teach the beliefs, behaviour, words and attitudes liked by Allâhu ta'âlâ, worships to be performed, and ways of attaining happiness in this world and in the Hereafter. Illusions and imaginary stories fabricated by the imperfect human mind are not called Din. Mind is useful in learning and obeying the religious commandments and prohibitions. Yet it cannot grasp the mysteries, the ultimate divine causes in the commandments and prohibitions. Nor can it reason on them. Such occult facts can be learned if Allâhu ta'âlâ intimates them to Prophets or inspires and reveals them to the hearts of Awliyâ. And this, in its turn, is a blessing that can be bestowed only by Allâhu ta'âlâ.

Now, attaining happiness in this world and the next and deserving love of Allâhu ta'âlâ requires being a Muslim. A non- Muslim is called kâfir (disbeliever, unbeliever). And **being a Muslim,** in its turn, requires **having îmân** and **worshipping. Worshipping** means adapting oneself completely to the Sharî'at of Muhammad 'alaihis-salâm', both in words and in actions. The prescribed worships must be performed only because they are the commandments of Allâhu ta'âlâ and without expecting any worldly advantages from doing them. The Sharî'at means the **canon** [commandments and prohibitions] taught in Qur'ân al-kerîm and explained through hadîth-i-sherîfs, and can be learned from what we term books of fiqh, or ilmihâl. It is **Fard-i-ayn** for everyone, men and women alike, to learn the Sharî'at, that is, the religious principles incumbent (to do or not to do) for every individual Muslim. These principles are remedies protecting men against spiritual and physical diseases. Learning medicine, arts, trade or law would take a person years in a high school and then years in a university. By the same token, learning the books of ilmihâl and the Arabic language requires studying for a number of years. People who do not learn these things will easily fall for the lies and slanders fabricated by British spies and by mercenary, hypocritical, and so-called religious men and treacherous statesmen misled by British spies, and will consequently end up in a disastrous and afflictive destination in this world and in the Hereafter.

Expressing **the Kalima-i-shahâdat** and believing in its meaning is called **îmân.** A person who expresses the Kalima-i-shahâdat and believes the facts purported by this word is called a **Mu'min** (Believer). The **Kalima-i-shahâdat** is "Ashhadu an lâ ilâha ill- Allah wa ash-hadu anna Muhammadan 'abduhu wa rasûluh." It means: "There is no ilâh (being to be worshipped) except Allah; and Muhammad 'alaihis-salâm' is His born slave and His Messenger whom He has sent to (guide) all humanity." No Prophet shall come after him. It is stated as follows in the Tahtâwî footnotes, at the end of the subject dealing with how to perform the daily prayers of namâz one has somehow missed or omitted, in the book **Merâq-il-felâh,** "Islam is not only believing that Allâhu ta'âlâ exists. Those disbelievers who attribute partners to Him believe in His existence, too. For being a Mu'min (Believer) it is necessary to believe that He exists, that He has attributes of perfection such as being One, being Alive,

Omnipotence, Omniscience, and Will, that He sees and hears all, and that there is no creator except Him." To believe that Muhammad 'alaihis- salâm' is the (Messenger=Prophet) means to believe that all his teachings were dictated to him by Allâhu ta'âlâ. Allâhu ta'âlâ revealed **Islam,** that is, îmân and the teachings of the Sharî'at to him through Qur'ân al-kerîm. The commandments to be observed are called **Fard.** Prohibitions are called **Harâm.** Altogether they are called **Sharî'at.** As soon as a person becomes a Muslim, it becomes fard for him to perform namâz (five times daily) and to learn the Islamic teachings commonly known among the people. If he slights learning them, e.g., if he says that it is unnecessary to learn them, he loses his îmân and becomes a **kâfir** (disbeliever). It is written in the 266th letter in our book **Müjdeci Mektuplar** that those who died as kâfirs will not be forgiven and will be subjected to an eternal fire in Hell. A person who loses his îmân is called a **murtad** (renegade). People who hold correct belief concerning the facts taught in Qur'ân al-kerîm and hadîth- i-sherîfs are called **Ahl as-sunna** (Sunnite Muslims). Allâhu ta'âlâ, being very compassionate, did not declare everything overtly. He expressed some facts in a covert language. People who believe in Qur'ân al-kerîm and hadîth-i-sherîfs but do not agree with the scholars of Ahl as-sunna in interpreting some of their parts, are called people without a **Madh-hab.** Of the people without a madh- hab, those who misinterpret only the teachings of îmân expressed covertly are called people of **bid'at** or deviated Muslims. Those who misinterpret the openly declared ones are called **Mulhids.** A mulhid is a disbeliever, although he may consider himself a Muslim. A person of bid'at, however, is not a disbeliever. Yet he will certainly be subjected to very bitter torment in Hell. Among the books which inform that Ahl as-Sunnat 'ulamâ are on the right path and are superior, the book **Mahzan ul-fiqh il-kubrâ** of Muhammad Suleiman Efendi, a virtuous Sudanese, is very valuable. On the other hand, kâfirs who pretend to be Muslims though they are not and interpret the overt teachings of Qur'ân al- kerîm in accordance with their own personal mental capacities and scientific information, and mislead Muslims, are called **zindiqs**.

Different scholars of Ahl as-sunnat drew different conclusions and meanings from the covertly expressed parts of the Sharî'at. Thus four different madh-habs appeared in matters pertaining to religious practices, that is, in adapting oneself to the Sharî'at. These madh-habs are named **Hanafî, Mâlikî, Shâfi'î** and **Hanbalî**. These four madh-habs agree in matters pertaining to îmân (belief). They differ slightly only in ways of worship. People who belong to these four madh-habs consider one another brothers in Islam. Every Muslim is free to choose and to imitate any of the four madh-habs and to perform all his deeds in accordance with that madh-hab. Muslims' parting into four madh-habs is the result of the mercy, the great compassion Allâhu ta'âlâ has over Muslims. If a Muslim has trouble performing a worship compatibly with his own madh-hab, he can imitate another madh-hab and thus do his worship easily. Conditions to be fulfilled for imitating another madh-hab are written in the (Turkish) book **Se'âdet-i Ebediyye** (Endless Bliss).

The most important worship is the namâz. If a person performs namâz it will be understood that he is a Muslim. If a person does not perform namâz it will be doubtful whether he is a Muslim. If a person values namâz and yet neglects it because of indolence though he does not have a good excuse for not doing so, the law courts of Mâlikî, Shâfi'î and Hanbalî madh-habs will give him death penalty, (if he is in one of these madh-habs). If he is in the Hanafî Madh-hab, he will be kept prisoner until he begins performing namâz regularly and will be commanded to perform all the prayers of namâz he has omitted. It is stated as follows in the books **Durr-ul-muntaqa** and **Ibni Âbidîn,** and in **Kitâb-us-salât,** published by Hakîkat Kitâbevi in Turkey: "Omitting the five daily prayers of namâz, i.e. not performing them in their prescribed times without any good excuse for not doing so, is a grave sin. Forgiveness for this sin requires making a hajj or tawba." And the tawba made for it, in its turn, will not be acceptable unless one performs the prayer, or the prayers, of namâz one has omitted. One must free oneself from this state of harâm by performing the omitted prayers of fard namâz instead of the daily prayers of sunnat namâz called Rawâtib. It is written in authentic religious books that if a person has debts of fard prayers of namâz none of his sunnat or supererogatory prayers of namâz will be accepted even if they are sahîh. That is, he will not attain the thawâbs (rewards), the benefits which Allâhu ta'âlâ promises (for performing supererogatory prayers). Their writings are quoted in our (Turkish) book **Se'âdet-i Ebediyye.** It is not sinful to miss a namâz for good reasons (prescribed by Islam). Yet all the four madh-habs agree that one has to perform as soon as possible any prayers of namâz one has missed or omitted be it with good excuses or not. In Hanafî Madhhab only, it would be permissible to postpone them as long as the time necessary for working for one's living or for performing the prayers of sunnat namâz called Rawâtib or the supererogatory prayers of namâz advised through hadîth-i-sherîfs. That is, it will be good to postpone the qadâ namâzes with these reasons. According to the other three Madh-habs, however, it is not permissible for a person who has debts of namâz omitted for good reasons to perform the so-called prayers of sunnat namâz or any sort of supererogatory namâz; it is harâm. The fact that the prayers of namâz omitted for good reasons are not the same with those neglected without good reasons is written clearly in **Durr ul-Mukhtâr, Ibni 'Âbidîn, Durr ul-Muntaqâ,** Tahtâwî explanation of **Merâk il-felâh** and **Jawhara.**

CPSIA information can be obtained at www.ICGtesting.com
Printed in the USA
BVOW08s0052230415

397261BV00017B/67/P

9 781910 220153